The Torah
A Beginner's Guide

"Well-conceived and well-written. A unique and fascinating venture that interweaves Jewish and Christian perspectives in a clear and careful fashion. It will no doubt launch further reflection on the part of both lay readers and biblical scholars."

Terence E. Fretheim – Elva B. Lovell Professor of Old Testament at Luther Seminary in St. Paul, Minnesota

"Clear yet not simplistic, sparing of detail yet opening a window into the vast world of Torah study for both Jews and Christians – this makes for a very welcome and highly useful book."

Ellen F. Davis – Amos Ragan Kearns Distinguished Professor of Bible and Practical Theology at Duke University Divinity School, North Carolina

"I am glad to welcome and commend this study guide for beginners. The authors show how the Torah continues to be a generative force for Jews and Christians."

Walter Brueggemann – William Marcellus McPheeters Professor of Old Testament Emeritus at Columbia Theological Seminary

"This serene exposition of the first five books of Jewish and Christian Scripture is most welcome."

Matthew Levering – Professor of Theology at the University of Dayton, Ohio

The Torah
A Beginner's Guide

ONEWORLD BEGINNER'S GUIDES combine an original, inventive, and engaging approach with expert analysis on subjects ranging from art and history to religion and politics, and everything in between. Innovative and affordable, books in the series are perfect for anyone curious about the way the world works and the big ideas of our time.

aesthetics	global terrorism
africa	hindusim
anarchism	history of science
aquinas	humanism
artificial intelligence	islamic philosophy
the bahai faith	journalism
the beat generation	judaism
biodiversity	lacan
bioterror & biowarfare	life in the universe
the brain	literary theory
british politics	machiavelli
the buddha	mafia & organized crime
cancer	magic
censorship	marx
christianity	medieval philosophy
civil liberties	middle east
classical music	NATO
climate change	nietzsche
cloning	the northern ireland conflict
cold war	oil
conservation	opera
crimes against humanity	the palestine–israeli conflict
criminal psychology	paul
critical thinking	philosophy of mind
daoism	philosophy of religion
democracy	philosophy of science
descartes	postmodernism
dyslexia	psychology
energy	quantum physics
engineering	the qur'an
the enlightenment	racism
epistemology	renaissance art
evolution	shakespeare
evolutionary psychology	the small arms trade
existentialism	the torah
fair trade	sufism
feminism	volcanoes
forensic science	
french revolution	
genetics	

The Torah
A Beginner's Guide

Joel S. Kaminsky and Joel N. Lohr

ONEWORLD
OXFORD

A Oneworld Paperback Original

Published by Oneworld Publications 2011

ISBN 978-1-85168-854-8

Typeset by Glyph International Ltd., Bangalore, India
Cover design by vaguelymemorable.com
Cover image by Joel N. Lohr with kind permission of
the Caven Library, Knox College, University of Toronto. © Knox College,
Toronto

Printed and bound in Denmark by Nørhaven

Oneworld Publications
185 Banbury Road
Oxford OX2 7AR
England

Learn more about Oneworld. Join our mailing list to
find out about our latest titles and special offers at:

www.oneworld-publications.com

Contents

Acknowledgements

This book has benefited immensely from the input of a number of readers, even if at times we opted to ignore elements of their sage advice. We want to thank especially Brad Anderson, Richard Briggs, Sandra Jacobs, Teresa Lohr, Walter Moberly, Mark Reasoner, Jody Rosenbloom, Christopher Seitz, and Anne Stewart. We would also like to express our deepest gratitude to Robert Hayward who helped organize and obtained funding to host a Jewish Studies Seminar at Durham University dedicated to the book. Further, we would be remiss not to thank both the Andrew W. Mellon Foundation and Smith College for providing various forms of funding that enabled us to collaborate in the writing process, and to obtain assistance to index the manuscript. Lastly, we are indebted to the team at Oneworld for the helpful suggestions that have greatly improved this work.

In this book we have striven to present an introduction to the Torah in a clear and accessible manner. The word *torah* itself is often translated as *instruction*, and much of the brilliance of the Torah resides in its ongoing ability to reach ever-new generations of readers. Our own knowledge of the Torah is due to the many fine teachers we have had. With this in mind we would like to dedicate this work to some of the most important mentors in our lives. Joel Kaminsky would like to dedicate his contributions in this volume to his two graduate school mentors, John J. Collins and Jon D. Levenson, as well as to his undergraduate teacher and advisor Harold O. Forshey. Joel Lohr would like to dedicate his contributions to his PhD supervisor R. W. L. (Walter) Moberly, as well as his undergraduate teachers Paul Edward Hughes and Craig C. Broyles.

Illustrations

A note to the reader

Throughout this work we refer to passages in the Bible according to a standardized convention which first indicates the biblical book, then the chapter number, followed by a colon, and then the verse number (or numbers). The books of the Bible can be found in the Table of Contents of most Bibles. In order not to overwhelm the beginner, we have kept biblical citations to a minimum; at times we use only one representative reference, and when possible we cite only the chapter without verse numbers.

There are a number of different expressions used to describe those books of the Bible that were originally written in Hebrew including: the Hebrew Bible (which *scholars* use to describe this collection); the Tanakh, Jewish Bible, or Jewish Scriptures (which refers to the same collection from a *Jewish* religious vantage point); and the Old Testament (a term used by *Christians* to describe the first part of the two-part Christian Bible, which contains a second major section called the New Testament). Because our discussion ranges through various contexts (Jewish, Christian, and secular), we use each of these terms when they are appropriate.

We have tried to define most other terms that might be unfamiliar to readers when we first use them. If you find that you need to be reminded of a definition, we have placed many important terms in our glossary near the end of the book. Also in the back of the book, the reader will find an approximate chronological timeline for the biblical period, and a host of further, suggested readings, organized by chapter. Our hope is that if you find certain topics to be of interest, these materials will help you explore them in more detail.

Finally, most of our translations of the Bible are drawn from the New Revised Standard Version. However, in places we use our own translation in order to convey the flavor of the Hebrew. Further, to put the reader in touch with the original biblical languages, on occasion we include important Hebrew and Greek words in a simple phonetic transliteration.

Abbreviations

BCE	Before the Common Era (equivalent to BC 'Before Christ')
CE	Common Era (equivalent to AD 'Anno Domini')
D	Deuteronomic Source
DH	Documentary Hypothesis
E	Elohist Source
J	Yahwist (or Jahwist) Source
JEDP	An acronym which combines the four literary sources of the Pentateuch
KJV	King James Version (of the Christian Bible)
NASB	New American Standard (version of the Christian) Bible
NIV	New International Version (of the Christian Bible)
NJPS	New Jewish Publication Society (version of the Jewish Bible)
NRSV	New Revised Standard Version (of the Christian Bible)
P	Priestly Source

Introduction
What is the Torah?

There is no question that the Torah is one of the most influential documents in Western civilization. It contains widely known characters like Joseph, Moses, and Noah, and archetypal stories such as the Garden of Eden, the Exodus, and the Golden Calf episodes. Its laws and teachings have shaped contemporary thinking and jurisprudence in profound ways. Further, Western art and literature have been and continue to be shaped by the Torah's powerful sway. Thus, it is essential for any intelligent reader – Jewish, Christian, Buddhist, Hindu, or secular atheist – to know the content of this seminal collection of texts. Despite this, audiences are frequently unfamiliar with many parts of the Torah and fewer yet have a clear sense of how the Torah's various pieces fit together.

Aside from the tremendous *cultural* influence the Torah has exerted, it is a profoundly *religious* document. Two of the world's major religions – Judaism and Christianity – consider the Torah to be sacred and to contain enduring truths about the creation of the world, the texture and meaning of human existence, and the nature and character of God. In fact, within both of these faith communities it is not uncommon to think of the Torah as a divinely given gift, even the very word of God. Although other parts may also be considered to be divinely inspired, the Torah is often understood to be the most important section of the Jewish Bible or Old Testament, something of a 'canon within the canon', that is, the most sacred subsection of the Hebrew Bible. Thus, understanding the Torah is also essential if one hopes to understand Judaism and Christianity.

But what exactly *is* the Torah? What do we mean by this term? The term 'Torah' most frequently refers to the first five books of the Bible, be it the Jewish, Catholic, or Protestant Bible. While the total number of biblical books and their order is distinct in these three traditions, all Jewish and Christian Bibles begin with the five books of the Torah in the same order: Genesis, Exodus, Leviticus, Numbers, and Deuteronomy. Scholars often refer to this collection as the Pentateuch, a word derived from the Greek term *pentateuchos*, meaning 'five scrolls' or 'five vessels'. Traditional Jews call the printed form of these five books the *Chumash*, a word derived from the Hebrew word for the number five. In popular parlance this collection is often called the Five Books of Moses. This latter designation likely arose both because Moses features prominently in these books and due to the traditional, longstanding belief that Moses authored them.

We should be clear that there is no title on this collection of books that names them 'The Torah'. In fact, the word *torah* only occurs once in the first book, Genesis, at 26:5 (it does occur later in the Torah). The Hebrew word *torah* can sustain a range of meanings including: teaching, instruction, law, procedure, principle, and so on. There are many instances in Leviticus where the word *torah* is used in a limited way to describe a specific ritual procedure (for example, Leviticus 6:2, 7, 18). The notion that the word *torah* might refer to a written book, or more accurately in antiquity a written *scroll*, likely arises from certain verses in Deuteronomy. Note, for example, the use of the term *torah* in Deuteronomy 4:8, where Moses asks the people: 'What other great nation has statutes and ordinances as just as this entire law [*torah*] that I am setting before you today?' Or, compare the language in the first half of verse 10 in Deuteronomy 30: 'When you obey the LORD your God by observing his commandments and decrees that are written in *this book of the law* ...' (more literally, *this scroll of the torah*). It is quite likely that originally these verses only referred to Deuteronomy or even just a part of the larger book of Deuteronomy. But once Deuteronomy was fully integrated into the first four books of the Bible, the references in Deuteronomy to a Torah scroll over time came to be understood as references to the full text of Genesis through Deuteronomy.

Within modern Jewish culture the word Torah is used to refer not only to the scroll containing the first five books of the Bible but it can be used to refer to any and all aspects of Jewish wisdom, lore, or law produced at any time from the Bible until today. Thus one might overhear the following conversation among two Jews, perhaps on a flight returning from Israel: 'How long were you in Israel? What were you doing there?' 'I was in Israel for six months studying Torah.' What the person who replied means is not that they were literally studying material in the first five books of the Jewish Bible but that they were studying Jewish religious texts of some sort. In fact, it is much more likely that such a person spent the bulk of their time studying the Talmud, a wide-ranging collection of rabbinic legal discussions, than reading the Pentateuch.

In the Christian tradition, the Torah is often called 'The Law', and sometimes this is contrasted with 'The Gospel'. The Christian tendency to think of Law and Gospel as opposing terms is largely due to sixteenth-century Reformation debates in Europe (particularly associated with Martin Luther), whereby salvation was believed to be obtained not through practicing good deeds or doing good works (that is, obeying the law) but rather was received freely through grace. The Greek word used in the New Testament for Torah, *nomos*, and its use elsewhere in ancient Greek literature, gives some credence to the idea of the Torah being an abstract set of principles or laws. However, judging by the way the word is used in the New Testament, the word *nomos* can hold multiple meanings as can *torah*, and not all are negative. Frequently in the New Testament this collection is simply called 'Moses' or the 'Book of Moses' and interestingly, when questioned, Jesus makes clear that obeying its teachings will result in eternal life (see Matthew 19:16–19; Mark 10:17–19; Luke 10:25–8). In some ways, we as authors hope to show what is meant by Jesus' teaching in these instances, as well as to highlight why he and Judaism more broadly regard the Torah to be life-giving, something also made clear in the Psalms of the Bible:

> Happy are those
> who do not follow the advice of the wicked,
> or take the path that sinners tread,
> or sit in the seat of scoffers;
> but their delight is in *the torah of the* LORD,
> and on *his torah* they meditate day and night.
> They are like trees
> planted by streams of water,
> which yield their fruit in its season,
> and their leaves do not wither.
> In all that they do, they prosper.
>
> (Psalm 1:1–3)

> Happy are those whose way is blameless,
> who walk in *the torah of the* LORD.
> Happy are those who keep his decrees,
> who seek him with their whole heart,
> who also do no wrong,
> but walk in his ways.
>
> (Psalm 119:1–3)

Although *torah* is often translated as 'law' in these passages, it is clear from the above that an abstract set of principles is not meant by this word. Rather, what is in view are real, practical teachings that lead to a full and upright life.

But now let us once more return to the focus of this book, which is an introduction to the first five books of the Bible. Typically students tend to think of the Bible as a single book and the Torah in some sense as the first large unified section of this big book. But the fact is that the Bible is actually a library of books. And while there is much that unifies the material in the Bible's first five books, the Torah contains a host of different kinds of material including mythic stories, genealogies, travel itineraries, census lists, many distinct types of narrative (ranging from the mundane to the miraculous, from very short to more lengthy and complex), poetic texts including prayers and prophecies to blessings and taunts, and legal texts dealing with criminal, civil, ritual, and ethical matters.

The story of the Torah covers some 2700 years beginning with the creation of the world and ending with the death of Moses and the Israelites now poised to enter the land of Canaan under Joshua's leadership. The basic storyline can be quickly summarized. Genesis 1–11 covers creation followed by several stories that describe the early history of humanity in rather negative terms. Genesis 4 relates the first murder, Genesis 6–9 the flood story, and Genesis 11 the Tower of Babel episode. In Genesis 12, things shift and the Torah begins to focus on one man named Abraham and his descendants, in particular his descendants through Isaac and Jacob. In fact the stories of Abraham, Isaac, Jacob (whose name is later changed to Israel), and Jacob's twelve sons (the ancestors of the twelve tribes of Israel) occupy the rest of Genesis. Furthermore, these chapters explain how Israel's ancestors ended up in Egypt, thus setting the stage for the dramatic miracles surrounding God's rescue of the Israelites from Egypt, described in Exodus 1–15.

Exodus 1 opens with a sudden turn in Israel's fortunes, as the Egyptians feel threatened by the prolific fertility of the Israelite resident aliens living in their land. Moses is born under this oppressive regime and his life is only preserved through a providential coincidence when he is found floating in a basket in the Nile and taken in by Pharaoh's own daughter. Forced to flee Egypt, God appears to Moses in a burning thorn bush and commissions him to work with God to free the Israelites from their bondage. After a series of escalating plagues and a miraculous escape from Egypt the Israelites journey to Mount Sinai.

Israel's stay at the base of Mount Sinai occupies a good portion of the Torah (Exodus 19:1 to Numbers 10:10, including all of Leviticus). It is at Sinai that God gives the Israelites the Ten Commandments along with many other laws by which they are to organize their communal life. The rest of Numbers describes Israel's journey away from Sinai toward the land of Canaan, including a few initial conquest stories of lands east of the Jordan River. Deuteronomy is in many ways a last will and testament of Moses in which he retells Israel's story from the Exodus to their current state in which they are camped on the edge of Canaan ready to conquer it. Here Moses also recounts many of the laws found earlier in the Torah, albeit with various innovations and refinements. Deuteronomy ends with a series of warnings and charges issued by Moses, followed by Moses' death and burial.

Our approach in this book

It may be helpful to think of this book as having two major sections. The first section, chapters 1–3, introduces essential background information on the Torah and how it has been read both religiously and academically. The second section, chapters 4–8, contains in-depth surveys of each book of the Torah. Each of these chapters concludes with specific examples of how the book under study has been used in both the Jewish and Christian traditions. We conclude with some brief reflections on how the Torah continues to influence society and religion.

This brings up two interrelated and important topics. The first is who we are as authors. Although we seek to present an impartial account of the above matters, we have no intention of hiding that we each stand, in some way or another, within the Jewish and Christian traditions (Kaminsky within Judaism, Lohr within Christianity). And while we have an interest in showing the continuing value of the Torah, this book is not an attempt to persuade readers to adopt our religious viewpoints, even if we hold to them with conviction. Our purpose is to describe and explain what the Torah is, how it has been and might be read, and why the Torah has been so influential religiously and socially. Here, however, a second issue comes into view, which we might call 'the ethics of interpretation'. As interpreters of the Torah we have attempted to strike a balance between reading the text sympathetically and at the same time critiquing aspects of the text that are indeed problematic from a contemporary viewpoint. We cannot hide or ignore the fact that at times reading this ancient literature is difficult. Although in places we provide strategies to overcome various difficulties in the text, we are also aware that certain aspects of the Torah will rightly remain troubling to a contemporary audience.

What follows is an attempt to shed light on the Torah in a manner that is accessible and engaging to contemporary readers. The book assumes no previous knowledge of this literature, hence the subtitle: 'A Beginner's Guide'. We invite you along for what should be an interesting, and hopefully productive, journey.

1
A few basics

Although it might be obvious to some, we should first note that the books of the Torah were not composed in English. Rather, the Torah is a Hebrew collection of writings. While it is possible that some of the stories and materials found in these books were originally handed down in another language (in an oral or written form), there is no known record of this; the Torah as we know it was composed and preserved in the language of the Israelite people in antiquity: Hebrew. What difference does this make?

There are two important matters to keep in mind here, the first of which applies to any translation. Firstly, what we read in an English translation of the Torah will always be one step removed from the original. This does not mean that we cannot understand or make use of a translated Torah, but given that at times the Hebrew Torah contains highly stylized language and in places poetic material, it is difficult to appreciate the nuances of the Torah fully in translation. We might say this compares to trying to read Shakespeare in German. Secondly, Hebrew presents some interesting challenges because in antiquity its written form included only consonants without vowels (the vowels were implied), making some words open to ambiguity. We will discuss both of these points, along with others, below.

Scrolls, language, and versions

While archeologists have recently discovered a sixth-century BCE silver amulet with an excerpt of Numbers 6:24–6 (the Priestly

Blessing), our oldest known *manuscripts* of the Torah are over 2000 years old and are part of an interesting story. In the late 1940s a collection of biblical, para-biblical, and sectarian (or religiously distinct) documents was found in the Judean Desert near the Dead Sea. This cache of documents, dating between 200 BCE and 70 CE, came to be called the Dead Sea Scrolls. Found by two Bedouin shepherds, these scrolls eventually changed hands, appeared for sale in 1954 in the *Wall Street Journal*, and were purchased by a party interested in their publication (they are now housed in the Shrine of the Book Museum in Jerusalem). It took many years, however, along with much controversy, before they were published and made available for scholars and others to examine.

The Dead Sea Scrolls contain fragments from every book in the Hebrew Bible except Esther and they are now the oldest existing biblical manuscripts. Like contemporary Torah scrolls, these ancient biblical books were composed using Hebrew consonants without vowels and were written in ink on parchment, that is, animal skins that have been cleaned, stretched, and dried. These biblical texts show some differences when compared with the standard Torah scrolls found in Jewish synagogues today (which are usually based on the Masoretic tradition; see below), though the variants are generally minor or provide clarification on well-known textual difficulties. The variations between manuscripts, however, suggest that one should think of Torah manuscripts as existing in families, families that share much in common with each other but ultimately go back to distinct unique forms of the Torah.

Let us re-emphasize that these differences in manuscripts generally involve only minor variations, mostly the occasional word change or incorrect letter, not huge inconsistencies or changes in the Torah's stories or commandments. However, it is often in the minor variants that scholars find interesting historical developments or theological slants. The science of determining the original wording of the text is called textual criticism, and

Figure 1 Dead Sea Scrolls fragment of Genesis 39:11–40:1, which narrates Joseph's encounter with Potiphar's wife. Photo Tsila Sagiv, courtesy Israel Antiquities Authority

this discipline uses a variety of biblical manuscripts in its task, Hebrew and non-Hebrew. For instance, in places in this book we will refer to the Septuagint, a Greek translation of the Torah and Hebrew Scriptures that dates before Jesus' time (between the third and first centuries BCE). There are Samaritan, Syriac, and

Aramaic editions of the Torah as well. All of this underlines the point we made above that there are several distinct families of Torah manuscripts.

The point to grasp here is that before one even begins to translate the Torah one needs to recognize that no matter how true one wants to be to the Hebrew, there is some variance within the ancient manuscripts that contemporary scholars consult when making their translations. Some of this variance relates to the fact that all manuscripts are copies of copies of even more ancient copies. Further, even the Hebrew in any single manuscript is open to a certain level of interpretive difference because, as mentioned, ancient manuscripts like those found among the Dead Sea Scrolls contain no vowels, may lack a full space between words, or may not contain punctuation or periods at the end of sentences. The lack of vowels (small Hebrew markings under and above consonants) can be seen in comparing the versions of Genesis 1:1 shown in figure 2.

בראשית ברא אלהים את השמים ואת הארץ

בְּרֵאשִׁית בָּרָא אֱלֹהִים אֵת הַשָּׁמַיִם וְאֵת הָאָרֶץ

Figure 2 Pointed and un-pointed Hebrew text of Genesis 1:1

This lack of vowels in early manuscripts sometimes allows for a single word to be vocalized in two or more different ways. One need only think of the letters *ctlg*, which can be vocalized in English as *catalog* or *cytology* or even *cat leg/cut log* if there was meant to be a space between letters. Of course, the act of translation itself always introduces additional elements of interpretation as one must decide whether to translate more literally or to translate more liberally, aiming to capture the spirit of the Hebrew text. For this reason, the reader might wish to consult different translations, such as the New Revised Standard Version (NRSV), the New Jewish Publication Society version (NJPS), or, for those wishing to get a sense of the actual Hebrew, the recent more literal translations by Everett Fox and Robert Alter.

THE MASORETES AND THE MASORETIC TEXT

The manuscript tradition that has long been regarded as the most reliable, at least until the discovery of the Dead Sea Scrolls, is called the Masoretic Text. This title is derived from the group of scribes called the Masoretes who meticulously preserved this tradition in the sixth to tenth centuries CE. These scribes are regarded as having developed the now common markings and vowel system around the consonantal text, seen in the pointed Hebrew excerpt in figure 2, called the Masorah. However, it is believed that these markings attempted to preserve older, often oral traditions of vocalizations and cantillations (markings indicating how the text is to be sung liturgically), as well as alternate spellings or other details such as how the reader should divide each verse. Particularly interesting is the care these scribes used in maintaining the Hebrew text through the centuries. Because there were no printing presses and the transmission of texts was done entirely by hand through careful checking and rechecking, these scribes devised a counting system in which every word and even every letter of each book of the Torah was accounted for and tracked. For instance, according to their calculations the Torah contained 400,945 Hebrew letters and the letter at the middle of the Torah was a *vav*, in the middle of the word *gakhon* (meaning *belly*), found in Leviticus 11:42. Such a system allowed scribes to count forward or backward from the start or end of a book to its middle, thus ensuring that not one letter was missing. It is not surprising, therefore, that when the Dead Sea Scrolls were compared to these much later manuscripts, very few errors or changes were found.

Who wrote the Torah?

The above helps us understand something of the nature of Torah manuscripts, the Torah's language, and how it has been preserved, but we have not yet addressed the question of who wrote the Torah. While this may sound like a straightforward, easy to answer question, it is in fact a very difficult one, one that scholars of the Torah can spend their lifetimes seeking to determine. For our purposes, there are two main positions to consider, and a third of more recent vintage: (1) the traditional view: Moses, under divine inspiration; (2) the Documentary Hypothesis, which suggests that a number of authors who lived well after Moses' time contributed pieces to the Torah; and (3) we cannot know for sure. However, because the second view will occupy a good portion of our discussion in chapter 3 on modern historical scholarship, we will only mention it briefly here in relation to the others. Readers can learn more about the Documentary Hypothesis in that chapter.

The Torah has long been associated with Moses and generations of Jews and Christians have regarded Moses to be its author. In Judaism before the time of Jesus, as well as in the New Testament, the books of the Torah are often called the 'Book of Moses', or the 'Law of Moses', or just 'Moses'. In some ways, claiming that Moses is the author of the Torah is also a claim of authority in that Moses was such an important figure in Israel's history and he had a special relationship with God. Not only did Moses meet with God face to face but the last chapter of the Torah states that Moses was uniquely gifted as God's spokesperson and that no such prophet has arisen in Israel since his time. Such a claim of authorship might thus be understood as an attempt to articulate the divine authority, and therefore credibility, of the Torah's teachings. In short, it makes a strong connection between the Torah and God.

Questions arise here because the author of the Torah is not mentioned in these books themselves. There are places where certain passages tell us that 'Moses wrote these things down', or that 'Moses spoke these words', and so on, but these are usually references to specific sections of the Torah. In truth, the work as a whole is anonymous. Further, the ancient practice of calling these books 'Moses' is not conclusive proof that Moses wrote them or that ancient authors are necessarily implying Moses wrote them in their entirety; it is quite clear that this convention simply associates Moses with the Torah rather than makes a statement about the Torah's authorship. To understand this, we only need compare those times when ancient authors refer to the Psalms as 'David', or to the Prophets as 'Isaiah'. Not only do we know that David did not write all of the Psalms, but we also know of instances where an author might indicate that a quotation is from Isaiah yet then quote from books that fall outside Isaiah itself. For example, Mark 1:2 introduces a quotation as coming from 'Isaiah' but then quotes not only from that book, but from another prophet, Malachi 3:1, as well. With regard to the Torah, even if Mosaic authorship could be shown, certainly some stories – particularly those in Genesis – must be much earlier than Moses and could only have been passed down to him by others in some form, likely oral. There are also stories or areas of the Torah that suggest another, later point of view; for example, Genesis 12:6 is written from the perspective of someone who lived long after Moses' time, in that it presumes that Israel had already conquered the land of Canaan. Furthermore, some texts of the Torah such as Numbers 12 and Deuteronomy 34 clearly include later reflections on the life, death, and significance of Moses.

Modern scholarship takes all of these concerns very seriously. It is also interested in the differences in language, vocabulary, and literary style of various sections of the Torah, and it seeks to understand how these differences might relate to questions of authorship. It is not that traditional Jewish and Christian interpretation was oblivious to or ignored these matters, because ancient Jewish and Christian interpreters regularly noticed and derived meanings from subtle and not so subtle shifts within the Torah's language. But modern scholarship took a different approach to them by seeking to understand the unevenness of the text through a historical lens. In a nutshell, the Documentary Hypothesis (the second view of the Torah's authorship) suggests that the Torah was not written by one author, but rather is a compilation of four main literary sources that were written by different parties over time. These sources were eventually compiled sometime after the Babylonian exile, around the fifth and fourth centuries BCE. Determining exactly which sources have been brought together and when, as well as the history, social setting, and transmission of these sources, is the work of source criticism, a branch of historical criticism. It is worth noting that affirming the composite nature of the Torah does not *necessarily* entail denying that it is divinely inspired. Just as the Christian New Testament is enriched by four distinct accounts of Jesus' life, death, and resurrection, so too can the composite nature of the Torah be viewed as something that adds depth and profundity to the text.

This brings up one last view on authorship. This third position, that we cannot know exactly who wrote the Torah, is a recent view that questions much of modern biblical criticism, most especially the quest to find the author or authors of the Torah. Despite the tremendous advances that such scholarship has made, and the important ways the Documentary Hypothesis has illuminated the history behind the Torah, some thinkers rightly note the problematic nature of trying to determine how the Torah was written. The expanse of time between us and the original author (or authors), and the fact that no single theory of authorship has been widely accepted like the Documentary Hypothesis once was, have caused these readers to conclude that we will never know with certainty how the Torah came about. Many scholars have thus suggested that instead of trying to determine the precise authorship of the Torah and its sources, our time and effort would be more productively spent reading and interpreting the Torah itself.

Conclusion

While we devote a substantial section of this book to explaining the Documentary Hypothesis as well as exploring questions surrounding the historical veracity of the Torah (chapter 3), we too recognize that in many instances time spent reading the actual text of the Torah is more productive than trying to determine the text's original authors and prehistory. Further, focusing too closely on the history of a text can serve to overshadow or even obscure the importance that such a text has had religiously, in this case for Jews and Christians. In the next chapter we explore how the Torah has been a part of and influenced both traditions down through the ages.

2

The Torah as a religious book

While historians and biblical scholars are naturally quite interested in the text of the Torah, the truth is that these books were carefully preserved over centuries because they are part of the Jewish and Christian bodies of sacred scriptures. As the first five books of both the Jewish and Christian Bibles, they received a great deal of interpretive attention from thinkers in both traditions and influenced each community's religious life. And, as noted at the end of this chapter, Islam too references many of the Torah's characters and stories.

Traditional Jewish interpretation of the Torah

Within Jewish tradition the Torah occupies such a central space that the term has come to take on two meanings. The first simply refers to the opening five books of the larger Jewish Bible, called the Tanakh. The term Tanakh is an acronym (TaNaK) that stands for *Torah* (Genesis–Deuteronomy), *Neviim*, the Hebrew word for Prophets (Joshua–2 Kings and Isaiah through Malachi), and *Ketuvim*, or the Writings (all the other books of the Jewish Bible). But, as noted in our introductory comments, in its more expansive meaning the term Torah can refer to any part, or all, of the vast trove of Jewish law and lore from antiquity to today. This dual usage is grounded in a larger rabbinic theory of the

Dual Torah. As we discuss in more detail below, the ancient Rabbis (or teachers of Jewish law and lore, who lived during the first few centuries of the Common Era) believed that Moses actually received two Torahs from God on Mount Sinai, one Written (the Pentateuch) and the other Oral (or Oral Torah). The Rabbis thus understand their own activities of interpreting and applying the Torah to new situations as simply making manifest aspects of the Oral Torah that Moses received at Sinai.

The centrality of the Torah can also be seen in how Jews understand the Torah's relationship to the larger Jewish Bible as well as in the disproportionate amount of commentary that later Jewish tradition produced on the first five books of the Bible. Within Judaism, the Torah is understood to contain God's revelation to his prophet Moses. The Torah itself asserts that Moses' place as one who speaks for God is pre-eminent. While the whole Hebrew Bible is viewed as sacred scripture, Judaism sees the Prophets and Writings as containing stories, prophecies, wisdom, and prayers of post-Mosaic Jews who sought to live their life according to the Torah of Moses. In fact, it is interesting to note that these other two sections of the Tanakh (Prophets and Writings) begin with strong injunctions to meditate on the Torah day and night (Joshua 1:7–8 and Psalm 1:2). The disproportionate attention that post-biblical Jewish tradition lavished upon the Torah can be seen quite clearly in the verse-by-verse commentary collections called midrash that the ancient Rabbis produced. Scholars speak of two major streams of midrashic writings: midrash halakhah, focusing on law, and midrash aggadah, focusing on narrative. The collections of legal midrash comment on the legal portions of Exodus through Deuteronomy. While there are collections of narrative midrash on biblical books beyond the Torah, a very large portion of these comment directly upon the narrative parts of the Torah.

The more abstract legal discussions found in the Mishnah and Talmud (both are early collections of rabbinic legal debates;

the Mishnah from around 200 CE, the Talmud building on the Mishnah composed between approximately 200 and 700 CE) do not directly comment in a verse-by-verse fashion upon the Torah. Nevertheless, the ancient Rabbis saw themselves as fleshing out the Oral Torah, which they believed Moses had received on Mount Sinai when he was given the Written Torah. In the rabbinic view, if one hopes to live in accordance with the revelation God transmitted to Israel through the prophet Moses, one needs both the Written Torah and the Oral Torah. This is because many of the laws in the Pentateuch are given in such terse form that it is difficult on the basis of just the Written Torah to understand exactly how to live in accordance with God's will. A quick example is the question of observing the Sabbath and keeping it holy. The Sabbath commandment in Exodus 20:8–11 clearly prohibits working on the seventh day of the week, Saturday, the Jewish Sabbath. Of course the question inevitably arose, what exactly constitutes work? What types of food preparation are permitted or prohibited on the Sabbath? Is one allowed to play sports or engage in other forms of recreation? Interestingly enough, while work is prohibited on the Sabbath, according to the Rabbis Torah study is not considered work and many observant Jews dedicate part of the Sabbath to such study. Much of the Mishnah and Talmud are devoted to illuminating and explicating these seemingly simple but in reality quite complex legal questions. Thus one very large volume of the Talmud is dedicated to unpacking the regulations surrounding keeping the Sabbath, several other tractates explore the rituals and meaning of certain specific biblical holidays (for example, there is a volume dedicated to Succot, the Festival of Booths, and another to Passover), and yet others focus on somewhat unusual biblical laws like that surrounding the ritual procedure for dealing with a suspected adulterer, mentioned in Numbers 5.

The Oral Torah was also seen as containing much of the back-story that helps one understand the often cryptic narratives in the

Torah and enables one to unpack their meaning. There are many ways the Rabbis engage in extracting further narrative details from the Written Torah. The important point is that they derive their interpretive insights from a very careful reading (some would say an *over*-reading) of the Hebrew text of the Torah. Often rabbinic interpretation is based upon unusual word usage, whereby the Rabbis fill in certain narrative gaps, or attribute significance to the juxtaposition of various passages. And it can involve highly creative measures such as *gematria*, a system that explores the numerical significance of various letters and words in a particular biblical passage (since each Hebrew letter has a numerical value), and then uses this to shed light on a story's meaning.

THE RABBIS INTERPRET THE BURNING BUSH

In Exodus 3, the Rabbis pick up on the fact that immediately before God appears to Moses, Moses is said to be shepherding Jethro's sheep. They then elaborate on this fact to demonstrate that it was the way in which Moses tended Jethro's flock that drew God's attention to choose him to lead God's own flock, the people of Israel. In fact, they note that David too was a shepherd and they illuminate his unique shepherding qualities as well. The Rabbis are quite intrigued with why God chose to appear to Moses in a desert bush. Here they suggest a host of possibilities including the rather profound insight that this occurred 'to teach you that no place is devoid of God's presence, not even a thorn-bush'. But they also note that the numerical value (or *gematria*) of the word 'the bush' in Hebrew is 120 and they suggest that perhaps God cryptically informed Moses of the length of his lifespan, 120 years, the figure given in Deuteronomy 34:7.

Rabbinical methods of reading the Torah place such a high value on the text that multiple approaches are necessary to unpack its full value. When one examines the ongoing Jewish tradition, which stretches over many centuries up to today, one quickly discovers that much of Jewish philosophical, mystical, legal, ethical, and theological thinking is preoccupied with attempting to understand and further elaborate upon the Torah, continually finding innovative and ingenious ways for the text to speak to a new generation living in a different historical context. Thus even today, contemporary Rabbis regularly discuss how to apply the Torah's ancient rules to our quickly changing, highly technological society. Examples abound from issues involving when abortion and organ donation are permissible to whether pre-programmed elevators may be used on the Sabbath. Furthermore, the vast post-biblical Jewish interpretive tradition regularly preserves not only differing but at times conflicting lines of interpretation. But this in fact carries on an ancient and venerable tradition that reaches back to the Torah itself, a point we highlight in our evaluation of the varying and at times conflicting accounts one finds in the text of Genesis.

The liturgical use of the Torah in Judaism

The word liturgy refers to the rituals practiced and the readings used in religious settings. There is evidence found within the Hebrew Bible as well as within the New Testament that portions of the Torah functioned liturgically in that they were read aloud in ancient communal religious gatherings. For instance, Deuteronomy 30:9–13 reports that every seven years 'this Torah', likely referring to some form of the book of Deuteronomy, is to be read aloud to the whole community at the Festival of Booths (or Hebrew Succot). Acts 15:21 implies that excerpts from the Torah were read on Sabbaths in synagogues. The exact scope and regularity of the ancient liturgical use of the Torah remain unclear. However, by the early medieval period one finds two cyclical patterns to complete the reading of the Torah within Judaism: a Palestinian one that took three years and a Babylonian one that completed the cycle in a single year. The tradition of reading through the entire five books of the Torah in a single year eventually became dominant. Thus when a Jew today walks into almost any synagogue in the world on a given Sabbath (or in traditional synagogues on Mondays and Thursdays as well), he will find that the Torah reading (or *lection*) for that week is identical to the portion being read in his or her home synagogue.

In this now widespread annual liturgical cycle, the Torah is divided into 54 portions, and each Torah portion, or *parashah*, is in turn paired with an excerpt from the prophetic books, called the *haftarah* (though the prophetic lection can vary in Ashkenazic and Sephardic synagogues). Because some of the standard weekly readings are displaced by Jewish holidays or the changing length of the Jewish lunar year, certain weeks may end up with double Torah portions. This in turn enables the community to complete the reading of the Torah in time for the annual celebration of Simchat Torah ('rejoicing of the Torah') that occurs at the end of the Festival of Booths each fall. While certain Reform and Conservative congregations have attempted to reintroduce a modern version of the triennial cycle in which they read only one-third of each weekly portion, the third that they read is drawn from the same lectionary portion read in more traditional synagogues. Thus, if one walked into a synagogue on the first week of the annual cycle one would hear either all of Genesis 1:1–6:8 being chanted (this recital is guided by a cantillation system, which is several hundred years old), or possibly one-third of that lectionary portion. The following week one would hear either all or one-third of Genesis 6:9–11:32. Each weekly excerpt is named after a Hebrew word or phrase that occurs in the opening verse of the lection (for example, the first is called *Bereishit*, the first word of Genesis meaning 'In the beginning'). Frequently, after the Torah is read, a congregant or the Rabbi will deliver a *devar Torah* (literally: a word of Torah), a sermon that explores the meaning of the weekly Torah portion.

Upon walking into a synagogue, the casual observer will notice that the focal point of the synagogue is a decorative cabinet, the ark. This ornamental closet houses the Torah scroll or scrolls owned by that particular community (see figure 3). Each scroll contains a complete copy of all five books of the Torah in a traditional, ornamental Hebrew script. A Torah must be handwritten by a scribe (in Hebrew a *sofer*), who is specially trained in the rules concerning the production of Torah scrolls, upon parchment that comes from the properly prepared skins of certain animals. The writing of a Torah scroll may take many months to produce and must not contain any scribal errors; this lengthy and involved process means that each community's Torah scroll is a valuable – and much cherished – possession. When the ark is opened, one quickly notices that every scroll is clothed in ornate fabric and frequently the scrolls have silver breastplates and crowns placed on the tops of the wooden poles to which each end of the scroll is attached. Before and after the Torah service the scrolls that are used are paraded through the congregation in a reverent and celebratory fashion. On the annual festival of Simchat Torah, congregations engage in extended dancing with the Torah scrolls owned by the community.

The liturgical practices surrounding the reading of the Torah reveal a number of widespread rabbinic theological assumptions about the meaning and significance of the Torah for Jews. For instance, when a congregant is called to the Torah they recite a blessing both before and after each part of the lection is chanted. In particular, note the following phrase from the blessing one recites when a section of the lection is concluded: 'Blessed is the Lord our God, King of the universe, who has given us a Torah of truth, and has planted everlasting life in our midst.' A life that is dedicated to the practice of the Torah's commands and the study of the meaning of the Torah is seen as a key

Figure 3 Torah Ark, Adath Israel Synagogue, Lower Merion Township, Pennsylvania. Courtesy Thomas Neely

to obtaining immortality. This is yet further expanded in the rabbinic propensity to equate the notion of 'Wisdom' – which the book of Proverbs speaks of as bestowing long life upon those who seek it – with Torah. Thus as the congregation returns the Torah scroll to the ark, words from Proverbs 3:17–18 are recited, which speak of Wisdom as 'a tree of life for those that grasp her' (Wisdom and Torah are both spoken of with feminine gender terminology).

The Torah has also shaped a host of other aspects of Jewish liturgical practice. Traditionally Jews pray three times a day and have an additional service added on Sabbaths and holidays. The daily, Sabbath, and holiday prayer cycle is based upon the sacrificial system described in Leviticus. Interestingly enough, some streams of Jewish tradition derive the practice of an afternoon prayer service from Isaac's meditative late afternoon walk in Genesis 24:63. A central aspect of the prayer service is the *Shema* which includes the closest thing Jews have to a creedal statement concerning God's unity, drawn from Deuteronomy 6:4–9; 11:13–21 and Numbers 15:37–41. The first two of these passages are also included in phylacteries, leather prayer boxes worn during weekday morning prayers (see figure 11), as well as in every *mezuzah*, miniature scrolls often placed in metal or wood boxes that are mounted on door-frames in Jewish households and buildings (see figure 4).

The bulk of the Jewish annual holiday cycle is tied to practices described in Leviticus 23 and Deuteronomy 16, including a number of festivals that are directly linked to what might be described as the honeymoon period when God began to interact with Israel as a people. Thus the yearly holiday cycle begins at Passover, which celebrates God's redemption of Israel from Egypt. The next holiday is Shavuot (or the Festival of Weeks), which by the early rabbinic period is linked to the giving of the law at Mount Sinai. The festival associated with blowing the *shofar*, the ram's horn, is tied to the Jewish New Year (Rosh

Figure 4 Example of a *mezuzah*

Hashanah) in the rabbinic period. Yom Kippur or the Day of
Atonement, discussed at length in Leviticus 16, is the holiest
day of the Jewish liturgical year. On this day, the community
fasts and prays that God may forgive the sins of each individual
and the larger community as he seals the yearly fate of all living
souls on this day. Succot, the Festival of Booths, is celebrated
in remembrance of Israel's wandering in the wilderness. Even
today, many Jews build temporary huts in their yards and eat (and
sometimes sleep) in them during this festive fall holiday. It should
be mentioned that Sabbath observance, one of the most repeated
ritual commandments in the Torah, is actually the first holiday
mentioned in Leviticus 23, a holiday that occurs each week!

We would be remiss not to at least mention the vast array
of Jewish ritual, ethical, and legal practices that are derived

directly from the Torah or indirectly from practices exhibited by characters (including God) within the Torah. Thus male circumcision, a longstanding Jewish practice, is drawn directly from Genesis 17 in which God issues this commandment to Abraham and his descendants. When God visits Abraham immediately afterward in Genesis 18:1, the Rabbis use this text to emphasize that visiting the sick is so important that even God visited Abraham as he was recovering from his circumcision. Similarly, the Rabbis stress the importance of clothing the naked and burying the dead by noting that the first act God does for Adam and Eve as a couple is to clothe them (Genesis 3:21) and the last act he does for Moses at the close of Deuteronomy is to bury him. Thus the Torah is not simply an ancient text that describes Jewish origins, but rather is the continuing focal point of contemporary Jewish practice as well as the touchstone of ongoing theological reflection.

Traditional Christian interpretation of the Torah: the New Testament

Because Christian interpretation of the Torah has changed so much over the past two millennia, it may be instructive to survey some of this interpretation down through the ages beginning with the New Testament. By beginning with the New Testament, a collection of writings generally regarded to be the earliest Christian literature (the books of the New Testament are generally dated to between 50 CE and 110 CE), patterns can be observed that affect later Christian interpretation. Following the New Testament, we will explore some methods of interpretation in the early Church Fathers as well as in the medieval and Reformation periods. This survey highlights a few of the Torah's major themes and trajectories while illuminating some of the similarities and differences in how Jews and Christians approach and interpret the Torah.

Although his relationship with the Torah is complex, it is clear that for the Jesus of the gospels the books of Moses held a very high authority. When asked what one must do to inherit eternal life, Jesus immediately replies that one must keep the commandments of Moses, usually summarized through quotations from the Ten Commandments or repetition of the *Shema* and what we today call the Golden Rule (found in Mark 10, and Luke 10 and 18). When challenged on certain commandments of the Torah, Jesus appears to have been aware of other schools of Jewish interpretation and he uses similar rabbinic principles in his explanations. For instance, when asked about divorce in Matthew 19, Jesus views the matter quite stringently and appeals to the language found in the Genesis creation story, judging that what God has brought together as 'one flesh' humans are not to separate, except in instances of infidelity. Here Jesus appears to side with the stricter interpretation of a contemporary Jewish teacher, Shammai, over the more lenient teachings of Hillel, another of Jesus' contemporaries, who permitted divorce in certain other circumstances.

Perhaps more interesting is Jesus' teaching on the law in Matthew 5–7, the 'Sermon on the Mount'. Here Jesus contends that he has not come to abolish the Torah's teachings and that not one jot or tittle (small Hebrew markings) will disappear from the law until 'all is accomplished'. Jesus does not make observance of the Torah simpler or easier to follow but instead he 'ups the ante', so to speak. For instance, while in the Torah adultery and murder were previously limited to physical acts – sleeping with another person's spouse or ending a person's life – Jesus teaches that if a man lusts over a women, or hates his brother in his heart, he has broken the commandments as well.

While in the New Testament Jesus often observes various commandments of the Torah, in some stories Jesus seems to challenge the validity of certain laws found in the Torah. Thus in

Matthew 12 Jesus and his disciples are accused of breaking the Sabbath and in Mark 7 he is accused of not maintaining purity laws stringently. When challenged on his practice in these areas, Jesus argues that the interpretation of the teachers questioning him is in error; that is, the teachers misinterpret the Torah. For instance, when challenged on picking wheat on the Sabbath in order to eat, Jesus maintains that his practice is in accordance with the essence of the law. When questioned about eating with hands that have not been ritually washed, Jesus states that the teachers of the law have misread and added to the Torah, making it more difficult than it really is. Despite his teaching, it seems unlikely that Jesus broke major Jewish food laws (compare the words of his closest disciple Peter in Acts 10:14).

Finally, to cover one last aspect of Jesus' use of the Torah, we should note that in the post-resurrection narratives of the New Testament gospels, especially Luke, Jesus begins a long tradition of Christian scriptural interpretation. Here Jesus makes use of the Torah (and the Prophets) to explain to his disciples that he is the long-promised anointed one, or messiah. The story of the Road to Emmaus found in Luke 24 is probably our most important example. Although his two disciples do not recognize Jesus while with him on the road, Jesus, 'beginning with Moses and all the prophets…interpreted to them the things about himself in all the scriptures'. Using the Torah (and Prophets) to argue that Jesus is the messiah will come to be a pattern in the early Church, as we shall see.

It might be argued that prior to Paul, followers of Jesus were Jews who observed the teachings of the Torah. It is really with Paul that we see the distinctives of the Christian religion (vis-à-vis Judaism) come to life: Non-Jews (or 'Gentiles') are brought into the Christian community and ritual observance of the Torah comes to an end (at least in large part). Paul's interpretation of the Torah is complex because of these developments and because he appears to have believed that Jesus' final return to establish his kingdom was close at hand and there was thus a limited time to bring Gentiles to God.

Paul's training as a Pharisee (mentioned in Philippians 3 and Acts 22–3) probably affected his interpretation of the Torah more than is often realized. To be sure, Paul's views regarding observance and non-observance of the Torah are radical, but his methods of interpretation share many similarities with those of the rabbinical schools in which he had likely been educated. For instance, in a controversial passage in Galatians 3, Paul proceeds to use the Torah itself to argue that it is not one's observance of the Torah that determines one's position before God. Paul makes use of the Genesis story in which God called Abraham before the giving of the law to argue that Abraham believed in the promise and his *faith* (not law keeping) is what justified him – that is, made him right with God. Paul then quotes Genesis 15:6 to make his point, arguing that those who have faith like Abraham (not keepers of the Torah) are Abraham's true children.

To demonstrate that the promise of Abraham is for all people through Jesus (Jew and non-Jew), Paul, in rabbinical fashion, makes much of a singular noun 'seed' used in various Genesis passages. This noun, usually understood to be a collective singular indicating a plurality (like the modern use of the word 'offspring'), is rendered as 'descendants' in most translations (for example, Genesis 12:7 or 13:15). In Galatians 3:16 Paul claims that God's promise was made to 'Abraham and his *seed*' (not seed*s*), and the seed is one person, Jesus. In this reading, Paul contends that the central promise of the Torah is not for Abraham's actual descendants but for all of those who profess faith in Jesus, the promised *seed*. Although elsewhere in 2 Corinthians 11 Paul reads the term 'seed' in the plural as 'descendants', here Paul makes use of a rabbinic principle in which texts of the Torah are read closely in order to exploit all possible meanings, even when such a reading is at odds with the natural thrust of the passage at hand.

Paul argues that reading the Torah rightly is a matter determined by metaphorical blindness or opening of eyes, the latter of
which happens through faith in Jesus. Probably most contentious
here is a passage in which Paul argues that the veil Moses
wore when he returned from Mount Sinai in Exodus 34 is
symbolically what keeps his fellow Jews from understanding the
Torah properly. According to Paul in 2 Corinthians 3, turning
to Christ permits one to see that the law is now made complete
in Jesus, and that it can only be read in light of him.

Paul's larger idea that spiritual light enables proper reading
of the Torah came to be of great significance for the Church
down through the ages, though Paul's views that the law was
made complete in Jesus (and thus no longer applies in practice)
certainly created its share of problems. As we will see, many of
these problems arose when the Church tried to make sense of the
fact that certain laws and teachings of the Torah must still apply
while others do not, and that the now 'faded' Jewish law was
still scripture, part of an important body of texts that it argued
pointed to Jesus as the messiah.

Traditional Christian interpretation
of the Torah: the Church Fathers
and beyond

It might be said that much of what propelled early Christian
interpretation of the Jewish scriptures in general and the Torah
in particular was an implicit acknowledgement that finding
references or allusions to Jesus in this literature is a complex
and difficult process. It is also clear that a great deal of this early
interpretation was affected by a growing concern to understand
how Christianity related to the Judaism from which it parted
even while it viewed the Torah and other Jewish scriptures as
authoritative.

Despite Christianity's origins as a Jewish sect, questions eventually arose as to whether the Christian community would retain the Torah and the rest of the Tanakh as scripture, and, if so, how these books were to be interpreted. Second-century debates with Marcion, an early Christian bishop later deemed heretic, are telling and ultimately resulted in an agreement to retain the Jewish scriptures as part of Christian scripture. For Marcion, the Jewish scriptures were incompatible with Christianity as he understood it: incompatible with grace, with Paul, and with Marcion's (shorter) version of a New Testament. The God of the Old Testament was not the God of Jesus, he argued; rather, the Old Testament deity was legalistic, tribal, and barbaric. The early Church rejected this dichotomy and it is largely through the subsequent teachings of the early Church Fathers, especially Irenaeus, that the Jewish scriptures came to gain acceptance as part of a two-fold canon within Christianity. Although the exact shape of the canon we today call the Christian Bible would not come for another two centuries, the early Church Fathers established the enduring significance of the Law and Prophets for Christians through models of interpretation that combined an allegorical approach with reading through a specific Christian Rule (or creed) of Faith.

The allegorical method used by many in the early Church is premised upon the idea that texts have hidden meanings, or mysteries, that need to be uncovered and explained. Texts may seem to have an obvious or plain sense but they often mean something else or have a deeper meaning that needs to be revealed. Although the method was not entirely novel (the first-century CE Jewish interpreter Philo also utilized it), in the early Church it was used in conjunction with the belief that *Christians* held the key to unlocking the mysteries of the Jewish scriptures. It was believed that the most reliable interpreters of this sacred literature were those in communion with Christ, particularly those teachers who succeeded from the apostles.

THE CHURCH FATHERS INTERPRET THE BURNING BUSH

The fourth-century Church Father Gregory of Nyssa had a particular interest in allegorical interpretations of the Torah, especially regarding the life of Moses, on which he penned a book. A characteristic example of allegory can be seen in his handling of the story of Moses and the Burning Bush (Exodus 3), in which Moses is instructed by God to remove his sandals. Here we quote from John O'Keefe and Russell Reno's *Sanctified Vision: An Introduction to Early Christian Interpretation of the Bible* (p. 101):

Gregory explains, 'That light [of the burning bush] teaches us what we must do to stand within the rays of the true light: Sandaled feet cannot ascend that height where the light of truth is seen, but the dead and earthly covering of skins, which was placed around our nature at the beginning when we were found naked because of disobedience to the divine will, must be removed from the feet of the soul.' Gregory is linking the narrative of the burning bush to his understanding of the human condition. Relying on Genesis 3:21, where God is depicted as making 'garments of skin' with which to cover the fallen Adam and Eve, Gregory interprets the sandals or 'coverings of skin' as a code phrase for the body of sinful desires that clothe our lives. Thus, Gregory's allegorical interpretation of the narrative of Moses shows us that our carnal desires make it difficult for us to correctly perceive God. Sandaled feet cannot ascend.

It was not too long before another school of Christian interpretation arose, in some ways in reaction to the allegorical method. The allegorical method was connected with interpreters from Alexandria (northern Egypt), but those who began to approach things differently – placing more emphasis on the literal and historical senses of the text – came mostly from Antioch (southern Turkey, today called Antakya). Although this newer 'Antiochean method' emphasized literal meanings of the Torah, it too was interested in extrapolating moral lessons from the Torah and it shared a concern with the allegorical approach to read the Torah through the Christian Rule of Faith.

FINDING JESUS IN THE TORAH

Because of the Bible's authoritative status within Christianity, it has often been used apologetically, that is, as a way to challenge an opponent's views or to prove one's point. This is true in Christianity today, and it was true in the early Church. In fact, one might say that the majority of early Christian writings are answers to opponents of the Church or arguments about particular Christian doctrines.

The debates regarding the pre-existent and divine nature of Jesus provide some of the most interesting apologetic uses of the Torah. The fourth-century Church Father Athanasius employed the Torah to prove that God and Jesus were both together from the beginning. In his reading of Genesis 1:26, where God states, 'Let us make humans in our image', Athanasius argues that God is speaking to Jesus who was present in the creation of the world. Later in Genesis 19:24, Athanasius, paying close attention to the text, determines that both God and Jesus were responsible for the destruction of Sodom. In that verse it states that 'the Lord rained on Sodom and Gomorrah sulfur and fire from the Lord out of heaven'. The curious double use of the word 'Lord', each one of whom (he argues) sends distinct forms of punishment ('sulfur' and 'fire' respectively), is seen by Athanasius to refer to two Lords: Father and Son (Athanasius, *Against the Arians*, 2–3).

The Antiochean method of interpretation paved the way for Christian interpreters like Jerome who translated the Latin Vulgate from the Hebrew text. He too was concerned to render the literal sense of scripture, even while he could simultaneously make use of the allegorical method. Eventually, the concern for the 'literal sense' of the text would culminate in one of

Christianity's greatest theologian–philosophers, Thomas Aquinas. This medieval theologian is especially important not only for his philosophy and emphasis on the literal sense in interpreting scripture, but also for his way of reading the Torah and its commandments. He is usually credited with formulating (though not necessarily inventing) a three-fold categorization system regarding the Torah's commandments. Aquinas argued that all Torah commandments could be categorized as moral, ceremonial, or judicial. According to this system, the Torah's moral laws are types of natural law, those that are eternally binding; the Torah's ceremonial laws are those that regulated Israelite worship of God, now obsolete; the judicial laws of the Torah regulated human relations and were regarded as derived from the moral law. Because God was now worshiped in Christ and judicial laws were simply ancient applications of the moral law, it was only the moral laws of the Torah that were still binding. Deciding what constituted a moral law – as opposed to a ceremonial or judicial one – came to be part of the interpreter's task.

With the Renaissance and the Reformation arose a host of changes in Christian interpretation, particularly because of these movements' emphasis on 'returning to the sources' (that is, returning to the original texts in their own language, without the filter of tradition). This development eventually gave rise to modern historical criticism, as we will discuss in chapter 3. Although massive changes took place, Aquinas' tripartite division of the Mosaic Law largely remains in force in Christianity today. A practical result of Aquinas' teaching was a renewed emphasis by the Reformers on the importance of the moral laws of the Torah, particularly the Ten Commandments, and this in turn came to affect the Christian countries of post-Reformation Europe as well as those countries founded by European nations, such as the United States and Canada. Remnants of this can be seen in the United States where the Ten Commandments still adorn various public spaces and courtroom walls today. This emphasis on the moral law also shaped how the Torah was used in Christian worship and catechism, a topic to which we now turn.

The liturgical use of the Torah in Christianity

It is difficult to separate the liturgical and religious use of the Torah from traditional Christian interpretation. This is primarily because those who penned early Christian texts on the Jewish scriptures were also churchmen – bishops or presbyters – those who taught and served in liturgical settings. What we find in the writings of the Fathers is probably not far from what local congregants heard in early church meetings.

However, to give the impression that meetings in the early Church involved little more than 'four bare walls and a sermon' would be entirely misleading. The early Church continued certain early Jewish synagogue practices such as delivering homilies or sermons based upon scriptural readings (including the Torah), and the recitation of various prayers and psalms. Additionally these meetings included early Christian hymns, collective confessing of creeds, baptism of new believers, and, most importantly, partaking in the Eucharist (a communal meal of bread and wine, signifying Jesus' broken body and shed blood). Over time, Christian meeting places came to be adorned with visual art that celebrated the life and death of Jesus as well as the ancestors of the faith, including the major figures of the Torah. These important pieces of art served to point the illiterate masses to live in the examples of the ancestors of the faith.

It is interesting to note that in the early creeds of the Church – those still recognized by almost all Christian churches today (for example, the Apostles' and Nicene Creeds) – there is no direct reference to the Torah, the Patriarchs, the Exodus, or Israel, though they do reference God as the 'Creator of Heaven and Earth'. There is some evidence to suggest that this important reference to God as creator not only is a direct allusion to Genesis 1:1 but is a shorthand way of referring to Israel's scriptures and history. This idea would likely have been assumed by the Church Fathers through their acceptance, and regular use, of the Old Testament. However, because this assumption can no longer be taken for granted, important voices have recently argued for the need to address the significance of Israel's story as presented in the Torah in Christian creeds and liturgies, and some changes to liturgies (though not yet creeds) have taken place.

Christian catechism often included teachings related to or derived from the Torah. Catechism itself arose out of a need to instruct new and young members of the Church in things related to Christian faith. These summaries of Christian doctrine often took a simple question-and-answer format which, when memorized, could be used when a new member was quizzed by the priest prior to baptism. The exact content of early Christian catechisms is difficult to ascertain but it is likely that these included sayings of Jesus, portions of the Rule of Faith, and teachings from various New Testament epistles; there is also evidence that these included basic teachings of the Torah such as monotheism and the repudiation of idolatry. Later catechisms – such as those named Catholic, Luther's, Heidelberg, and Westminster – usually include extensive sections explaining the Ten Commandments.

From accounts of early baptism ceremonies, we know that often these services included the use of the Torah, particularly those stories that involved water such as Noah and the Flood and Israel's Exodus from Egypt. These stories served as models for the new convert. Just as Noah was saved by passing through the

waters of the flood, and as Israel was saved by God in passing
through the Red Sea, so too was the recipient of baptism said to
be saved by God through the waters of baptism.

The Torah has featured strongly in Christian lectionaries.
Modern lectionaries are usually geared toward reading through
large portions of the Christian Bible over the course of one
or three years. These are structured so that each worship
service includes a reading from the Old Testament, the Psalms,
the New Testament epistles, and the four gospels. In most
Eastern and Western Christian lectionaries there is provision
to read from the Torah, though large portions (especially of
Leviticus and Numbers) are often left out. It is interesting to
note that although many Protestant churches do not use the
one- or three-year cyclical lectionary, there is sometimes a
provision to read 'The Law' (often the Ten Commandments)
in weekly worship services. This is especially true in churches
closely aligned with the Reformation, such as Lutheran and
Calvinist, where the Ten Commandments might be read each
Sunday by the minister. At times, however, Jesus' summary of
the law found in passages such as Matthew 22:37–40 is read
instead.

If truth be told, although modern Christian scholarship engages with the Torah and the Old Testament in serious ways, the
contemporary Church often neglects or overlooks the Torah
in its day to day life. Though the Torah may occasionally be
used to teach moral lessons based on the Patriarchs, or might
be used to show God's faithfulness in delivering the Israelites
from Egypt, the place of the Torah in the Church has at times
become auxiliary at best. Even in worship settings where the
lectionary ensures that the Torah is read, pastors and priests
often struggle with its application to contemporary life. The
complexities involved in reading the Torah as Christian literature
make this understandable. However, it is hoped that some of
the materials in the present book might provide an entry point

for Christians hoping to understand the Torah's relevance to their faith.

The Torah in Islam

The Qur'an, the sacred scripture of Islam, generally recognizes the authority of both the Jewish and Christian scriptures for Jews and Christians, but Islam believes that aspects of these two scriptural bodies have been distorted in ways that the Qur'an has not. The Arabic equivalent of the word Torah is mentioned in the Qur'an, although at times it seems to function as a designation for the whole of Jewish scripture rather than specifically the Pentateuch. Interestingly, the Qur'an mentions many of the same characters found in the Torah, including Adam, Cain, Abel, Noah, Abraham, Lot, Isaac, Ishmael, Jacob, Joseph, Moses, and Aaron. The Qur'anic stories surrounding each of these characters frequently share common elements with the Torah's storyline but just as often the two documents diverge from each other in important ways.

EXCERPT FROM THE QUR'AN: THE STORY OF CAIN AND ABEL

... tell them the truth about the story of Adam's two sons: each of them offered a sacrifice, and it was accepted from one and not the other. One said, 'I will kill you', but the other said, 'God only accepts the sacrifice of those who are mindful of Him. If you raise your hand to kill me, I will not raise mine to kill you. I fear God, the Lord of all worlds, and I would rather you were burdened with my sins as well as yours and become an inhabitant of the Fire: such is the evildoers' reward.' But his soul prompted him to kill his brother: he killed him and became one of the losers.

(The Qur'an, Sura 5:27–30,
translated by M. A. S. Abdel Haleem)

> **EXCERPT FROM THE QUR'AN: THE STORY OF CAIN AND ABEL (cont.)**
>
> Interestingly enough, in the above excerpt from the Qu'ran the name of each brother is missing. Further, the Cain-like character announces his intent to kill his favored brother who in turn responds by indicating that God accepted his sacrifice for a reason. Neither of these details is recorded in the Torah's version of this narrative.

While Islam does not view the Torah as authoritative for Muslims, the Qur'an and the Torah share some narrative as well as larger conceptual elements (for instance, a shared emphasis on worshiping only the one true God). Of course the divergences between the Torah and the Qur'an should not be overlooked or underestimated, and our purpose here is not to suggest a congruence of viewpoints as much as to provide some understanding of how the Torah and the Qur'an might relate to each other. In short, while one can clearly see affinities between the Torah and the Qur'an, it may be less useful to speak of a common Judeo-Christian–Islamic culture or heritage because doing so glosses over important religious differences, as well as the fact that Jews and Christians consider the Torah to be part of their authoritative scriptures while the Islamic community does not.

Conclusion

Having given an overview of the way in which the Torah has been interpreted and used religiously by various communities, in the following chapter we will provide an outline of some important modern 'secular' approaches to the Torah. Both religious and secular approaches to the Torah often notice similar problems in the text, but they approach them through differing frameworks. In fact, as discussed below, some of the more recent holistic approaches to the Bible build upon the insights of ancient traditional interpreters who tried to make sense of the Torah as a whole.

3
Modern approaches to the Torah

Whole books have been written on the various modern interpretive approaches to scripture. Our purpose here is not to be comprehensive but to provide a basic overview of a few contemporary approaches. For those who would like to explore these or other approaches in more detail, we have included a number of suggestions for further reading at the end of this book.

The Torah and the historical-critical approach

The historical-critical approach seeks to determine what we can know about ancient texts in the light of their history, literary sources, and parallel ancient documents, as well as in the light of the communities that wrote, heard, and used these texts in the ancient world. This is done in order to interpret the text more competently. Although at times this approach has become synonymous with the more narrow discipline of determining the authorship of the Torah, the approach in fact involves much more, especially regarding the historical background of the Torah. In this section, we look at two important aspects of historical-criticism in relation to the Torah: (1) the modern critical theory regarding who wrote the Pentateuch (the Documentary Hypothesis), as well as (2) how history and archeology relate to the Torah and its stories.

The foundation of all modern critical study of the Torah is the Documentary Hypothesis, a theory which seeks to explain the origins of the Torah. As mentioned in chapter 1, this theory arose out of the long-noticed differences in language, vocabulary, and literary style of various sections of the Torah, as well as references in the text that seemed to be later additions or were anachronistic.

The hypothesis was largely founded upon the work of a French medical doctor in the eighteenth century, Jean Astruc, and it was further developed and popularized by Julius Wellhausen, a Protestant German biblical scholar of the late nineteenth century. Wellhausen focused not only on the differences in language and literary styles in the Torah but he also aimed to explain various tensions, contradictions, and differences of outlook that one finds in the Torah. For example, as noticed by many before him, Genesis 1–2:3 contains a seven-day creation story, which describes God as transcendently creating the world in an orderly and patterned manner, culminating in the creation of humankind followed by God's resting on the Sabbath. Yet, beginning in Genesis 2:4 one finds a second creation story that varies in that Adam is created early in the process and in turn the subsequent creation of the animals takes place for him. In fact, Adam names all the creatures as each one is created and brought to him. To give another example, in the flood story of Genesis 6–9, some verses such as Genesis 6:19–20 describe Noah bringing two of each animal on to the ark while others such as Genesis 7:2–3 speak of seven pairs of clean animals and a pair of all other animals. Further, there is some confusion regarding how long the flood lasted. In Genesis 8:1–5 the duration of the flood is 150 days, while in Genesis 8:6 (and elsewhere) it lasts 40 days and nights.

Wellhausen's Documentary Hypothesis (DH from this point forward) was an attempt to give a comprehensive explanation of this unevenness in a clear, logical, and scientific way. The DH posits that the Torah was not written by one person but was woven together from four major sources in a lengthy and complex process. Tensions in the text are thus attributed to the compilation process that drew these sources together and thus created various inconsistencies. Although Wellhausen did not invent the labels J, E, D, and P – letters which signify the four sources underlying the Pentateuch – he adopted these and linked each source to a particular historical context in ancient Israel. Much of the persuasive power of this theory (and thus Wellhausen's fame) comes from the fact that it not only seeks to explain tensions in the Torah, but it also puts forward a model of Israel's evolution as a people or nation. For example, the D source corresponds to the book of Deuteronomy (hence the letter 'D'), a book that contains specialized vocabulary and appears to have been produced during the seventh century BCE by scribes who wanted to reform Israel's religion (as indicated by 2 Kings 22–3). So, although Deuteronomy is presented as the last will and testament of Moses, the DH contends that it actually reveals more about seventh-century Israelite society than about the much earlier time of Moses in which it is literarily set.

Inasmuch as D came to be associated primarily with Deuteronomy and seventh-century Judah, the other four books preceding Deuteronomy thus contain materials belonging to J, E, and P, designations we will explain in more detail below. The following text box presents a short introduction to the names of God in the Torah. These names are used in distinguishing the J and E sources.

THE NAMES OF GOD

The Hebrew Bible refers to God by several different words and names. For example, God is regularly referred to as *Elohim,* the generic Hebrew term for God. There are other names used of God as well. Thus God is sometimes referred to as '*El*', usually occurring with a second word such as *El Shaddai* ('God-Almighty') or *El Elyon* ('God-Most-High'), and so on. Most of these divine names

THE NAMES OF GOD (*cont.*)

are reasonably straightforward. However, one deserves special attention: God's personal name, YHWH.

God's personal name YHWH is used twice as often as *Elohim* and more than any other divine name, some 1800 times in the Torah. It is written using four Hebrew consonants: *yod*, *heh*, *vav*, and *heh*, or in English transliteration Y – H – W – H. Scholars often call this the Tetragrammaton, a Greek word simply meaning 'four-lettered word'. In English Bibles, this name is most often substituted with a reverential title, written in small capital letters: LORD.

While modern critics have put forward various proposals for how one might properly pronounce the Tetragrammaton, in traditional Judaism the personal name of God has long been considered too sacred to utter in casual circumstances. In fact, there are good reasons to believe that it was considered too sacred even to write. For example, from the religious community at Qumran (who produced the Dead Sea Scrolls), there are manuscripts that show empty spaces (or in places four raised dots) where it is clear that the divine name YHWH should be present. These manuscripts at times also contain the divine name in an ink and script different from the main text. This may indicate that a more senior scribe performed the task of inserting this sacred name after the initial production of the scroll (see figure 5).

Historical evidence suggests that although Jews more generally stopped pronouncing the Tetragrammaton at some point, the name was still pronounced during Yom Kippur by the high priest in the temple, likely spoken over the people in a blessing (probably during the recital of the Priestly Blessing of Numbers 6:24–6). Even this practice fell out of use, perhaps finally at the destruction of the second temple in 70 CE, though it is not easy to confirm the specific contours of this history. It is interesting to note that in early Christianity – itself a Jewish sect in the first century – Christians did not pronounce the name of God and readers may be surprised to know that Jesus himself is nowhere recorded to have used the personal name of God, whom he usually called 'Father' or 'Lord'.

Figure 5 Dead Sea Scrolls Fragment showing Psalm 121. Arrows point to examples of the name of God being omitted and written in a different script. Photo Clara Amit, courtesy Israel Antiquities Authority

Wellhausen, along with others, noticed that a fairly unified set of materials, particularly found in Genesis, used the divine name YHWH. He called this set of materials J, standing for JHWH, since there is no consonant Y in German. Thus the J source is the only source in Genesis to use the four-letter name of God, YHWH. Wellhausen believed that the J source was the earliest of the Pentateuch's sources, dated to sometime around 850 BCE, and that it originated in the southern area of Judah (rather than Israel, a name originally used to designate the northern ten tribes). According to the model, J uses vivid, concrete, and humanlike language in its descriptions of God and in its storytelling.

The letter E in the DH stands for the Elohist source, the source that used '*Elohim*' to refer to God within Genesis. E often provides alternative versions of J stories, and at times this source appears to be reacting to J. Here it was suggested that E often tried to 'correct' J in that it used less humanlike language and was more reverential in its descriptions of God. Wellhausen dated this material around a century later than J (sometime in the 700s BCE) and suggested that it was the product of the northern kingdom, Israel. A very brief example of the two sources sitting side by side can be glimpsed in Genesis 30:23–4 in which Rachel gives two different explanations for why she named her firstborn son Joseph. In the first she uses *Elohim* and proclaims that 'God has taken away my reproach' (*asaf elohim*). In the next verse, however, she explains the name using YHWH (rendered as LORD in English translation): she says, 'May the LORD add to me another son' (*yosef yhwh*).

P stands for Priestly, and the remaining material in the Torah fell into this category. This P material is grouped together by the fact that the vocabulary and interests of this material is priestly, likely penned by ancient Israelite priests. Thus the DH attributes the first, more orderly, creation story to P in that it culminates in the Sabbath, a sacred occasion that involved specific rituals important to priests. Leviticus, a book centered on questions of purity and sacrifice, is also attributed to P. In Wellhausen's theory, P is the latest source, dating to around 450 BCE, and he believed that this last source was added to J, E, and D to complete the Torah around 400 BCE, after Israel's exile in Babylon.

It is here that Wellhausen's particular evolutionary scheme becomes most intriguing but perhaps most troubling and biased. Wellhausen believed that P was the latest source because he thought religions developed in a common pattern whereby a preferable spontaneous religion (as in J) became rigid and ritualized at a later stage (as in P). Thus Wellhausen assumed that because P is preoccupied with ritual, it in turn must correspond with the latest and least inspired period of Israel's history. It is likely that Wellhausen's German Protestant background, which favored a 'heart religion' over 'deeds religion', shaped his views of P being the latest, and least inspired, source. While many scholars today recognize that Wellhausen correctly identified a unique Priestly body of material in the Torah, many view ritual as a vibrant religious impulse, which in fact may have flourished much earlier in Israelite history.

The historical evolution of the Torah according to the traditional DH is summarized in figure 6. The DH was the subject of a long-running scholarly consensus that has all but completely broken down in the past few decades. While virtually every scholar would agree that the Torah is composed of different sources, many scholars disagree with the DH's proposed dating. Further, recent scholarship has shown that the material of the Torah is much more unified than the DH acknowledged. Truthfully, it is not as easy to delineate these theoretical sources as was formerly thought. Nevertheless, it is clear that when one looks closely at the Hebrew texts of the Torah, it is hard to escape the conclusion that various sources have been brought together, however complex that process might have been, and however difficult it is to determine the exact way that process unfolded.

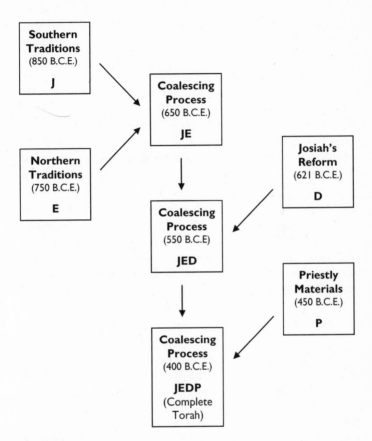

Figure 6 Diagram representing the traditional Documentary Hypothesis

Although matters of the Torah's composition are complex, they pale in comparison to issues raised in trying to make sense of whether the stories we encounter in the Torah are historical. Did characters like Adam, Noah, Abraham, and Moses actually walk the earth? Did Israel's departure, or 'exodus', from Egypt really happen? Did all the people of Israel really hear God speak to them from Mount Sinai? These questions are not easily answered and those who attempt to read the Torah's narrative as a straightforward linear, historically accurate report will quickly notice a number of problems. Where did Cain find his wife? Did someone named Noah really build an ark that could hold two of every land animal on earth? Is it really possible that Abraham twice attempted to pass off his very aged, but apparently beautiful wife as his sister (compare Genesis 12 and 20) only to have Isaac do this again in Genesis 26? If Ishmael was already thirteen years old in Genesis 17, why does he appear to be a very young child in Genesis 21? Such examples could be greatly multiplied.

Rather than seeking to report events in a historically linear and accurate fashion, the Torah appears to be more concerned to illuminate events from a religious perspective. This can be seen through a discussion of Hebrew names. Even a cursory survey of names in the Torah shows that they function as more than simple terms of reference. Adam, which in Hebrew means 'man', 'human', or 'creature', comes from the Hebrew term *adamah*, which means 'ground' or 'earth', the very substance from which the first human was created according to Genesis 2. Genesis 3:20 relates Eve's name to the Hebrew verb *chayah*, 'to live', and she is said to be the 'mother of all living'. Cain's name might mean 'created' or 'acquired one' (the first human 'created' by Eve), while Abel's name is simply the Hebrew word for vapor, vanity, or meaninglessness. The list goes on including Seth ('replacement', for his brother Abel), Noah ('refuge', or 'comfort', seen in the flood story but also perhaps in his wine-making activities; compare Genesis 5:29 and 9:20–1), Abraham ('father of a multitude'), Sarah ('princess'), Ishmael ('God heard'), Jacob ('supplanter'), Israel ('wrestles with God'), Moses ('drawn one/one who draws out', that is, from the water), and so on. The matter may seem trivial until one comes to ponder the fact that Adam, 'earth creature', and Eve, 'mother of all living', are said to have had a son named 'meaninglessness', whose life is snuffed out quickly by his brother.

Things become even more complicated when one considers that Hebrew, the language in which these names acquire their meaning, was not developed until a much later time (around 1400–1200 BCE). Would the first human being really have been named *adam*, or his son *hevel* – distinctly Hebrew names – even though the language was not developed until much later, a few thousand years after the stories' implied settings?

This is really just the tip of a very large historical iceberg. There are also problems related to archeology and the Torah. Although we should respect the saying that 'the absence of evidence is not evidence of absence', it is troubling that archeology has little to show for people like Abraham, Joseph, or Moses, who one would think were important people in the ancient Middle East given the length of their stories in the Bible and the roles they are said to have played in Egypt. Although the archeological record fits well with later Israelite history, like that of later Israelite kings (for which some stone inscriptions do exist), there is widespread agreement among scholars that there is no direct archeological evidence for the Patriarchs, for Moses, for the Exodus, and some would even say for later figures such as King David. What do we make of this lack of evidence?

There are generally two camps in these debates, which scholars often call 'minimalist' and 'maximalist'. It is probably safe to say that no one in either camp would self-identify with such a label and it is probably also true that the majority of biblical scholars fall somewhere in between. So-called minimalists are generally skeptical about anything that cannot be shown through external evidence, usually archeological data outside of the Bible. Thus, because the only record we have of Abraham and Moses is from the Bible itself, their stories are labeled as ideologically driven fictions, the creation of fifth-century scribes hoping to convince Israelites living in Babylon to repopulate the land of Canaan, and to contribute to their new temple. Certainly, such thinking goes, there would be some record of a people leaving Egypt in such a magnificent way – given that Egyptians kept extensive histories – or there would at least be some archeological evidence for Israel's large-scale entrance into Canaan through their alleged conquest. Maximalists, on the other hand, are often accused of taking the stories of the Torah at face value and reading them with a 'the Bible says it, I believe it, and that settles it' approach. However, maximalists rightly note that many details in the Torah fit broadly into an ancient Near Eastern context, dating well before the exile of Judah in 587 BCE. Furthermore, some parts of the Torah comment upon and challenge other portions of it, likely suggesting a longer writing process than many minimalists allow. In any case, the debates become polarized and too often practitioners in both camps talk past each other when in fact they have much to contribute to each other, especially given that there are thoughtful, careful, and important voices on both sides.

As we can see from only a few examples, there are a multitude of complexities involved in relating the Torah to history, as well as in determining the Torah's authorship. Nevertheless, in spite of various limitations, historical study of the Bible more generally, and of the Torah in particular, has surely advanced our understanding of this literature more than we would have thought possible two or three centuries ago.

The Torah and feminist interpretation

The rise of modern scholarship has also contributed to greater attention to the Bible from scholars engaged in feminist and gender studies and a good deal of this attention has been focused on the Torah, especially on the book of Genesis. Here one should point out that there are many different types of feminist approaches ranging from those interpreters who think the Torah's views of women are destructive and beyond redemption, to those who read the text suspiciously yet think the picture is mixed, to those who argue that the Torah has a model view of women and in fact contains the rudiments of modern feminism. Although modern feminist interpretation began in the 1960s and became a major movement in the 1970s, it was the groundbreaking 1978 study by Phyllis Trible and her probing analysis of Genesis 2–3 in *God and the Rhetoric of Sexuality* that really propelled widespread interest in this type of reading. In particular, Trible showed how a careful reading of Genesis 2 reveals much greater balance between Adam and Eve than was often granted. One might contest elements of Trible's argument, but her insight that subsequent, more patriarchal interpretive traditions have distorted our ability to read what the text actually says is of enduring value.

HEBREW MATTERS: WOMEN AS 'HELPERS'?

Trible's discussion of the Hebrew term *ezer*, 'helper', used in Genesis 2:18, 20 to describe Eve's relationship to Adam touches on a number of often overlooked facts. It had long been assumed by most interpreters that if Eve is described as Adam's helper, she must be inferior to Adam. But Trible notes that the context of this story and the word itself point to something different. Not only does the story make clear that the man, Adam, is incomplete and lacking something to be remedied by the woman, but the Hebrew term *ezer* is not necessarily a pejorative one, and is sometimes used of God's own role. That is, God is at times described as the great helper in his relationship to humans or the people of Israel and clearly such usage is not intended to depict God as inferior to those he helps. Although not all agree, and the text may still reveal some gender imbalances, Trible makes a reasonable case that the English usage of 'helper' which implies one who is an assistant, or even a servant, distorts our ability to read what the Bible actually says about Eve's relationship to Adam.

While it is impossible to deny the strongly patriarchal character of biblical religion, it is equally unwise to deny that the Hebrew Bible in general and the Torah in particular contains complex portraits of a number of female characters including Eve, Sarah, Hagar, Rebekah, Rachel, Leah, Dinah, Tamar, Potiphar's wife, Pharaoh's daughter, and Moses' wife Zipporah. Adam, Abraham, Isaac, Jacob, Judah, Joseph, and Moses all at times find their lives shaped, and in places corrected, by powerful women.

Furthermore, at least a few of these female characters are set in stories that one could reasonably call proto-feminist in that such stories critique elements of Israel's patriarchal culture. One thinks particularly of the story of Tamar in Genesis 38. This narrative interlude within the Joseph tale relates the strange manner in which Judah's lineage, the important lineage that will eventually lead to David, is continued. The story begins by indicating that Judah obtains a wife, Tamar, for his oldest son Er who dies prematurely and childless. Through an ancient form of surrogacy, Tamar is betrothed to Judah's second oldest son Onan, so that Onan might produce a child who would be legally Er's heir even though biologically being fathered by Onan. But Onan engages in *coitus interruptus*, perhaps in self-interest to protect his own inheritance (producing offspring for his late, older brother likely meant forfeiting an inheritance), and thus he refuses to impregnate Tamar. God in turn kills Onan, once more leaving Tamar without a husband and Judah without a future heir. Judah decides to withhold his third son from Tamar because he assumes that Tamar must be responsible in some way for the deaths of his two older sons. The narrator, however, skillfully critiques Judah's patriarchal presumption of Tamar's guilt by attributing these two deaths to the sinful behavior of each man. Through a careful plan and audacious actions, the now disguised Tamar tricks Judah into impregnating her. Then Judah, the unknowing father, demands that Tamar be executed for committing adultery, inasmuch as she had sexual relations with a man other than Judah's third son to whom she was engaged. Immediately thereafter Judah is indicted by his shrewd daughter in-law and at the end of this clever story, Judah himself pronounces that Tamar 'is more righteous than I' despite her actions, which might appear (to a modern audience at least) deceptive and even licentious.

In a similar fashion, one senses that the wife-sister stories in Genesis 12, 20, and 26, along with the Dinah story in Genesis 34, provide a critique of how the patriarchal treatment of women distorts social relationships more generally, often leading to unnecessary social conflicts that sometimes result in bloodshed. Women in these stories are important, and when one moves to Exodus, things continue along a similar trajectory in that women are seen to be key to the story. The actions of three groups of women in the first two chapters of Exodus make clear in no uncertain terms that the revolt later led by Moses is only possible because various Israelite and non-Israelite women flouted Pharaoh's orders to kill every male Israelite baby at birth. That one of these women was Pharaoh's own daughter, and that her behavior in taking mercy on the crying infant is a direct imitation of God's own actions toward the innocent who cry out (see Exodus 22:21–7), highlights the value placed upon women. Critics will continue to argue over precisely how patriarchal the Torah is, or how one might assess the morality of certain specific women characters such as Sarah, Hagar, or Rebekah. But as seen in our treatment of the individual books of the Torah, there is no doubt that theological reflection on the Torah has been greatly deepened by recent attention to gender issues raised by the text.

The Torah and ideological and socio-political criticism

Ideological and socio-political criticism developed in reaction to the modern notion that one can objectively interpret texts without bias. These methods seek to expose the ideologies of the text by exploring the social and political reasons why the books of the Bible were written. Their assumption is that these texts were written in order to establish or maintain the power of specific groups. However, recognizing that ideology is not only a product of the past, these approaches also suggest that later interpreters who uphold these texts have ideologies as well and these groups or individuals *also* seek to establish or maintain power through their readings. Interpreting the text thus becomes concerned with how the author, original reader, and later interpreter all obtain, maintain, or take away power. As we shall see, and as others have suggested, an important problem can arise, however, in that these methods often lead to the conclusion that texts no longer have actual meaning, speak truth, or have continued relevance; rather, interpreting texts is reduced to questions about the struggle for – and maintenance of – power.

Despite this criticism, it is not difficult to demonstrate the usefulness of this method. For example, a number of critics have argued that the ancestral stories in Genesis 12–50 reflect concerns of a much later period in cryptic form. Thus several recent scholars have proposed that much of Genesis correlates with issues that would have been especially important to those exiles who were returning to Jerusalem after the Persians conquered Babylon in 538 BCE. Stories about Abraham, a character who begins his life in Babylon and journeys to Canaan, are viewed as mirroring the Persian context. In this case, such stories might reveal the wish of its writers to motivate those living in Babylon to return to their proper home, Judah, the land promised to Abraham in Genesis. Further, Abraham's various interactions with other groups living in Canaan are believed to set a paradigm for the Judean returnees, suggesting that they interact with those who currently occupy the land in ways similar to Abraham.

We can see, therefore, that this method can illuminate the context behind the text. However, there are at least three important ways that the method presents problems, one of which has been mentioned. First, even if one is able to determine the period in which something was written, it is not always clear that one can identify the exact ideological purpose for which a particular text was written. It is precisely this difficulty that is apparent in the example above that seeks to correlate a substantial block of Genesis to groups and events in the Persian period. Thus Mark Brett, in his recent book on Genesis, argues that the stories in Genesis reflect an openness toward foreigners and thus challenge certain exclusionary ideas found in other Persian era biblical texts such as Ezra and Nehemiah, which prohibit intermarriage. On the other hand, Christopher Heard, though agreeing with Brett that Genesis 12–36 dates to the Persian era, argues that the exclusion of Esau and Ishmael from Abraham's covenant is proof that these materials are ethnocentric and support the ideology found in books like Ezra and Nehemiah that advocate excluding those who may have intermarried. In short, these two scholars agree on the historical context in which much of Genesis was produced, but yet they reach opposite conclusions about the ideologies that reside within the text.

A second equally troubling difficulty is that a single passage can fit into a number of historical eras. This is so not only because much of Israel's history remains obscure, but also because over time a single passage may have been linked with a multiplicity of events. In fact, other critics like David Sperling correlate much of the Torah, including substantial portions of Genesis, with characters and events of the monarchic era, placing them hundreds of years earlier than the Persian period.

Finally, to reiterate a problem mentioned at the outset, the following quotation from Jon Levenson makes clear that a problematic assumption animates methods of this sort:

The popularity of this form of interpretation is owing in no small measure to the pervasive modern perception, found even among the devout on occasion, that the category of the sacred is a mystification of social and political arrangements. Responsible interpretation, then, is the task of reducing larger spiritual structures to the institutional arrangements that not only accompany them, but account for them. That such arrangements are real, important and likely to be missed by religious traditionalists is to be granted. What must not be granted is this quasi-materialist presupposition that the correlating of text with its social and political arrangements exhausts an interpreter's task.

(Levenson, *The Death and Resurrection of the Beloved Son*, 118)

In conclusion, ideological criticism is indeed useful for interpretation in that it forces us as readers to recognize the ideologies of the text as well as our own biases. Despite its usefulness, however, it also has the potential to leave one with the impression that texts are little more than interesting artifacts with ideologies that need to be exposed but ultimately overcome and left in the past.

Holistic approaches to the Torah: literary criticism

Dissatisfied with biblical scholarship's tendency to privilege the historical-critical approach – which focused on reconstructing the earliest sources that reside behind the text of the Bible – a number of scholars in recent decades have striven to read the biblical text in a holistic, literary fashion. Robert Alter, a literature professor from University of California Berkeley, helped propel this method forward with his widely influential book titled *The Art of Biblical Narrative*. In this work he time and again demonstrated that certain oddities in the text that historical critics regarded as evidence that the Torah had been haphazardly spliced together from multiple sources could just as well be explained on literary grounds. In many of his examples, Alter built upon the insights of traditional Jewish interpretation, interpretation that had long wrestled with the tensions in the text but saw these as contributing positively to a rich theological reading. Rather than attributing these textual tensions to conflicting accounts that stem from separate sources, both the ancient Rabbis and contemporary critics such as Alter assume that such variations produce a more complex narrative by creating ambiguities and representing the story from different angles.

Contemporary literary criticism, therefore, is concerned with the text itself rather than that which lies behind it (the world of the author, the circumstances that led to its composition, and so on). In short, literary criticism of the Bible is primarily concerned with things like literary artistry, plot, narrative development, literary characters, the implied reader, point of view, the effect of the narrator, use of key words or a *leitmotif* (recurring theme), and so on.

Here we will once more use the story of Tamar and Judah as an example of how one can glean significant insight into a textual tension that earlier source critics would have attributed to seemingly disparate sources (and thus separate stories) that have been spliced together in a clumsy fashion. Source critics usually see this story as out of place inasmuch as it interrupts the flow of the Joseph narrative, which begins in Genesis 37 and resumes in chapter 39. As we will see, literary critics agree that it interrupts the narrative but instead see this as integral to the larger story and its literary artistry.

Alter, building on ancient rabbinic commentary on Genesis, astutely observes that several Hebrew expressions link Genesis 38 to both the preceding and following chapters in the Joseph story, and that these links point to some significant additional thematic connections. In particular, he highlights that the Hebrew behind Tamar's expression 'Take note, please' found in Genesis 38:25 is identical to the expression found in Genesis 37:32 on the lips of Joseph's brothers who ask Jacob to 'take note, please' to see if he recognizes the torn garment as Joseph's. Unfortunately, translations like the NRSV obscure this connection by opting to render the two identical expressions quite differently. An additional verbal connection is found in Genesis 38:1, in which we are told that 'Judah went down', and Genesis 39:1, in which 'Joseph was taken down'. One quickly now begins to notice additional thematic links. While Judah allows himself to be drawn into an improper sexual relationship in chapter 38, Joseph rejects the sexual advances of Potiphar's wife in Genesis 39. In fact, Judah's behavior is uncovered when Tamar produces an item belonging to Judah, an act that resonates both with the garment produced by Joseph's brothers in Genesis 37 and with Joseph's tunic that Potiphar's wife retains and uses to impugn Joseph's integrity in Genesis 39. The close ties between Genesis 38 and the surrounding chapters not only allow one to compare Judah and Joseph, but also help one understand the way in which Judah's character begins to evolve and mature into the self-sacrificing Judah one finds later in Genesis 44. Additionally, by interrupting the flow of the Joseph story, Genesis 38 creates a time-lapse that allows the reader to feel that in the meantime Joseph has been journeying toward Egypt.

This type of close reading not only attends to connections between various related passages, but also to unusual features within a single passage. For example, in Genesis 38:15 Judah assumes the woman he has met on the road to Timnah is a prostitute (in Hebrew a *zonah*). Yet in verse 21 when his friend Hirah asks around concerning the woman Judah had intercourse with, he uses a different Hebrew word, *qedeshah*, often rendered sacred prostitute. It is difficult to know for sure exactly why this change in terminology has occurred, but many literary critics would see it as significant. One possible literary explanation is that Judah wished to obscure the fact that he slept with a regular prostitute by telling his friend Hirah he slept with a sacred or temple prostitute. Such an act may have been viewed as socially more positive. Of course one must entertain the possibility that these two differing words were simply used interchangeably in this instance. The larger point is that even though not every shift in Hebrew usage is significant, close attention to changes in vocabulary and style often yields interesting insights into the passage under discussion.

Interestingly enough, very careful attention to the Hebrew text is a characteristic that actually undergirds the historical-critical approach as well, though to historical critics such variations are frequently seen as evidence of different sources or different editorial layers of the text. But in a literary reading this attention to the Hebrew text is combined with a presumption that before fragmenting any story into its underlying components one should first do one's best to read the actual text as a unity since presumably the Bible had meaning for those who put it in its final form.

There are definite limits to literary approaches, and in some way the method is only truly functional when used in conjunction with the insights gleaned from other methods that might illuminate the historical background of a particular passage, a word's potential meanings, or a phrase's grammatical structure. Literary readings that ignore the historical context in which the Hebrew Bible was written at times misrepresent the Bible because they misunderstand its vocabulary or grammar, often by reading contemporary usages into it. Words change meaning over time, so the more one knows of the context of a usage, the easier it will be to understand a specific text properly. A contemporary English usage example is that supposedly the King of England complimented the architect Christopher Wren upon his completing St Paul's Cathedral in London by telling him he had 'wrought an awful and artificial structure'. If one did not know the seventeenth-century context one might assume that these words were an insult as they would be today.

Literary criticism, like each of the approaches we examine in this book, should be seen as one of the many tools in the interpreter's toolbox, and one that often complements other approaches. In fact, one could argue that the feminist approach often combines a close literary reading with insights garnered from ideological and historical criticism and that historical critics frequently attend to the same details literary critics highlight. Truth be told, many biblical scholars today regularly draw on all of these methods in an eclectic fashion, depending on the specific passage under discussion, in that different types of texts are illumined more by certain approaches and less by others.

Holistic approaches to the Torah: canonical

Literary criticism's concern for the text as we have it is in congruence with what is called a canonical approach, which appreciates that individual passages sit within particular biblical books as well as within a larger body of literature (whether within the Torah, the Hebrew Bible, or the larger Christian Bible). However, canonical critics would find a purely literary approach to the Torah unsatisfying inasmuch as literary critics often read the Torah as simply another piece of literature. A canonical approach takes as its starting point the fact that many who interpret the Bible stand within religious communities that accept the Bible as a canon of scripture. The term 'canon' (from *kanon*, a Greek word meaning 'rule', 'standard', or 'measuring stick'), used in biblical studies to refer to a set collection of writings deemed to be authoritative (in this case, the Bible), implies that texts within the canon carry religious authority. The canonical approach is thus interested in how this literature as a whole and its various parts speak to faith communities, both in church and synagogue.

This type of approach seeks to illuminate how certain books and passages in the Bible affect or are affected by one's understanding of other books and passages that share common content or ideas. Canonical scholars are also interested in why the canon contains the variety of books it does, how these books relate to each other, and whether there are unifying theological themes overall.

The canonical approach diverges from the historical-critical method in ways similar to the literary approach. While the historical-critical approach tends to focus on the historical backgrounds of a text – often trying to discover a text's original independent components or original forms – practitioners of the canonical approach have a theological concern with the text in its final form, the text as we have it in the canons of the Jewish, Catholic, or Protestant Bibles today. It places great significance on the final product and believes that the reasons why it has been brought together, in the form it currently is, are important *theologically*, even while it does not deny the prehistory of particular books or the extensive editorial activity that brought various sources together.

With regard to the Torah, the results of the canonical approach can be noticed in a number of important ways. For instance, canonical interpreters might ask why Genesis begins with a universal picture, rather than with, say, Abraham, Israel's first known ancestor. Or they might inquire as to why Deuteronomy ends with Israel not having entered the Promised Land – something that takes place in the very next chapters of Joshua. In other words, this approach is interested in how the shape of the canon affects the reader and the story of the Bible more generally. Regarding the first example, it might be said that the decision to start with all humanity in Genesis is an attempt to show God's concern for all humankind, making it the foundation for God's relationship with Israel. Or, to put it another way, God's story with Israel (initially Abraham) is in response to a larger universal human condition. Regarding the question about the ending of Deuteronomy, one effect of the canonical shape of the Torah is that because Israel is left in the desert at the book's end, the listening audience is guided to focus more on Deuteronomy's instruction than on the immediate conquest of the land. Including the account of Israel's conquest might have distracted from or placed less emphasis on Deuteronomy's commandments. These proposals may be contested and debated, but such debate illustrates the interests and possible fruitfulness of the canonical approach.

One difficulty this approach encounters is that although Jews, Catholics, and Protestants view a number of the same books as scriptural, they do not share a common canon. In fact, even while the Jewish Tanakh and Christian Old Testament share the same books, as we noted earlier these are in a significantly different canonical order, which affects how one interprets this literature. Additionally, the theological differences that separate various Christian denominations leave one wondering whether such an approach is capable of providing a meeting ground for these divergent traditions. Nevertheless this approach remains valuable in that it recognizes that many who interpret the Torah do so within the context of a particular faith community that sees the Torah as part of a wider body of sacred scripture and tradition.

Conclusion

It is now time to turn to a more detailed account of each book in the Torah. Should questions arise over our interpretation of a specific passage, readers are encouraged to consult that passage and decide for themselves if a proposed interpretation seems sound or not. This book is not an answer key, but rather an invitation to readers unfamiliar with the Torah to begin engaging with this wonderful and lively book.

4

Genesis

Introduction and placement in the Torah

By far the longest book in the Torah, Genesis contains some 1534 verses in 50 chapters. The name Genesis, meaning 'beginnings', is derived from the Greek Septuagint's title for the book. In Jewish tradition, the book of Genesis is called *Bereishit*, a title derived from the first word of the book in Hebrew, which means 'in the beginning'. Both titles are especially apt for the first few chapters, but they also apply to the entire book, as we will see. Not only is the creation of the world and humankind contained in these pages, but so too is Israel brought into existence.

Already in antiquity Jewish interpreters commented upon the oddity that the Torah, a book centered upon and preoccupied with the laws given at Sinai, opens with the lengthy set of stories one finds in Genesis. The *Mekhilta* (a Jewish halakhic midrash, or legal commentary, on Exodus) contains a reflection on the Ten Commandments that asks why these seminal commandments are not placed at the beginning of the Torah. Similarly, Rashi, the great eleventh-century Jewish Bible and Talmud interpreter, begins his commentary on Genesis by asking why the Torah, at heart a law book, does not begin with the first commandment given to the whole people of Israel, a command that occurs in Exodus 12:2. The *Mekhilta* answers its own rhetorical question with an insightful parable about how a king who wishes to rule over people must first do things to earn their respect; likewise God first redeemed Israel from Egypt and also provided manna and quails before asking for their allegiance. Rashi, on the other hand, sees Genesis as necessary so that other nations cannot claim that Israel simply stole the Holy Land. Since God has ownership of the entire world through his creation, he can choose to give Israel this piece of land at will.

Overview of Genesis

Scholars usually divide the book into two major sections, Genesis 1–11, called the 'Primeval History', perhaps better termed the 'Primeval Story' or 'Primeval Cycle', and Genesis 12–50, called the 'Patriarchal Narratives' or perhaps better the 'Ancestral Narratives'. The Primeval Story begins with the creation of the world and highlights God's formation – and thus ownership – of the earth and humankind. The story contains a number of 'what went wrong?' moments, events in the early history of the world that not only show an apparent downward spiral in human action, but a progressive change in God's dealings with humanity. Here God appears to be remarkably responsive and adaptable. This early material in Genesis 1–11 is more universal in scope, in the sense that it concerns all humanity and not only a specific people, something that shifts considerably in chapter 12.

Often referred to as the 'Call of Abraham', the narrative that begins chapter 12 might be seen as the climax of the Primeval Story in that it initiates a new era, an era that will engage – and hopefully mitigate – the problems of the past through this new figure and his children. However, this change in emphasis also brings about problems of its own, not least in how those who are not of Abraham's special lineage relate to God and those God favors. These narratives thus highlight the complex relationships between the chosen and those who stand outside the Abrahamic covenant.

The stories of Abraham, Sarah and Hagar, Isaac and Ishmael, Jacob and Esau, Rachel and Leah, and Joseph and his brothers dominate the Ancestral Narratives. The book eventually ends with Israel, now a small people, in Egypt.

Contemporary controversies

A number of important scholarly debates grew out of and in turn focus upon the book of Genesis. Some of these have been touched on in our section on the Torah and the historical-critical approach (chapter 3), so here we briefly look at one issue that seems to receive abundant popular attention: are the materials found in Genesis 1–11 historical, and if they are not, how are they best understood?

Truth be told, the issues of creationism and evolution generate little scholarly interest outside a small subset of those thinkers taking a very traditional or at times a fundamentalist approach to the text. The issues here are not as complex as some would have it, at least if one takes the genre of this literature seriously. Already early in the third century CE, the Christian interpreter Origen addressed similar questions in looking at Genesis 1–3. At the risk of endorsing his condescension in the passage, his words are worth recalling:

> Now what man of intelligence will believe that the first and the second and the third day, and the evening and the morning existed without the sun and moon and stars? And that the first day, if we may so call it, was even without a heaven? And who is so silly as to believe that God, after the manner of a farmer, 'planted a paradise eastward in Eden', and set in it a visible and palpable 'tree of life', of such a sort that anyone who tasted its fruit with his bodily teeth would gain life; and again that one could partake of 'good and evil' by masticating the fruit taken from the tree of that name? And when God is said to 'walk in the paradise in the cool of the day' and Adam to hide himself

behind a tree, I do not think anyone will doubt that these are figurative expressions which indicate certain mysteries through a semblance of history and not through actual events.

(*On First Principles*, 4.3.1)

In fairness, we need to acknowledge that the ancient shapers and readers of Genesis likely *did*, at a minimum, regard the earth to be relatively young. We also have no reason to believe that they viewed the creation of the earth to happen other than in the rather straightforward way Genesis 1 explains. However, close readers will also notice numerous complexities and disjunctions in the Genesis story, like those Origen mentions above, and it seems that these were not of great concern to the ancient audience. This suggests that the story was already read or heard in antiquity on a deeper – perhaps metaphorical – level. At any rate, it is probably safe to say that the creation narrative had a greater significance for ancient Israel than simply to explain how things came into being within 144 hours.

Most scholars regard much of Genesis 1–11 to be mythic in nature. In the field of religious studies the term 'myth' is not used the way it is popularly, that is, as signifying something false or made up as opposed to actual facts or history. Rather, scholars use the term to describe a type of story that communicates deep truths about the nature of human existence or about the human understanding of the divine. Myths contain profound truths even if they are open to question historically. Inasmuch as these mythic texts from Genesis are primarily concerned with exploring what it means to be human, why life and work are difficult, why humans die, and so on, scholars generally view the popular tendency to focus on 'creation science' or 'evolution and the Bible' as a fundamental misreading of this type of material. It would be akin to trying to ask scientific and historical questions about the story of 'Little Red Riding Hood' or asking literary questions about the list of ingredients on a cereal box. Here we are not implying that Genesis 1 falls into the same genre as either of these two examples, but rather are suggesting that one must correctly identify the genre of the material one is dealing with in order to know what types of questions one can or cannot pose to a specific text.

Other closely related ancient Near Eastern texts provide further support for understanding these materials as mythic. It is clear that the two creation narratives as well as the Garden of Eden and flood stories in Genesis share much in common with other ancient Near Eastern origin stories (for example, the Enuma Elish, the Epic of Atrahasis, and the Gilgamesh Epic). This is not to say that because these stories are all mythic that they all communicate exactly the same message. On the whole, the Hebrew Bible portrays humans in a much more dignified and exalted role. In the Enuma Elish, the ancient Mesopotamian creation epic, humans are created from the blood of the rebel deity Kingu to alleviate the workload of the lower gods. In this view, human life is an endless task of low-level servitude, with humans functioning as guest workers imported to do the chores that the lower divine beings find demeaning. In contrast, Genesis 1 depicts the first ancestors of human beings, both male and female, as created in God's own image and given dominion over the world.

Creation: Genesis 1–2

Genesis begins with two distinct creation stories. The first account (Genesis 1:1–2:4a), which is more theocentric (or God-centered) in orientation, depicts Israel's God as a transcendent creator who stands apart from the created order. These characteristics, along with its highly elevated language and almost hymn-like structure, have led most modern scholars to attribute it to the P, or Priestly, source. As mentioned above, this creation story reveals a great deal of continuity with the larger Near Eastern cultural context in which ancient Israel flourished. For example, unlike later Jewish and Christian readings of this story that assume creation out of nothing, here God neither creates the waters nor the dry land. Rather God puts each in its proper place.

HEBREW MATTERS: DID GOD CREATE THE WORLD OUT OF NOTHING?

Traditionally, Jews and Christians have affirmed the belief that God created the world from nothing and they have grounded this belief in the language of Genesis 1. However, many contemporary interpreters suggest that when translated properly, the first verses of Genesis do not assume that God created the world out of nothing. Genesis 1:1 may in fact be read as a summary statement (see the NRSV and NJPS translations). Here some confusion occurs because the Hebrew of Genesis 1:2 contains an expression describing the pre-creation world as in a state of *tohu vavohu*, often translated as 'a formless void'. But by using the word 'void' these translations reinforce a common misperception that the Israelites thought that no 'matter' existed before creation began. This exact phrase occurs only once elsewhere in the Hebrew Bible, in Jeremiah 4:23, and it is clear from that passage that this expression should not be rendered as 'void'. Rather, it might better be translated as topsy-turvy (or 'messy and chaotic'), in that it describes a scene of creation before it is shaped into an orderly and productive world by God or, in Jeremiah, a world that has been devastated due to God's coming punishment. But in both passages, certain raw materials exist within this undeveloped state.

Although some have blamed Genesis 1 for empowering humans to abuse the environment and other critics of religion at times blame the Bible for disempowering humans by its emphasis on their creaturely status, each of these polar readings overlooks the place humans are given in the Genesis 1 creation account.

Far from degrading humans, this passage comes close to deifying them. But it does not in fact give humans full divinity, reserving the right to create, and for that matter to *destroy* creation, only to God. This account is then capped with a notice that God saw that everything he created was very good, followed by a passage linking the seventh day (or Sabbath) to God's own rest from creating the world. As often noted by Jewish thinkers, one of the central points of the commandment to observe rest on the Sabbath is to recognize that God, not human beings, created and controls the universe.

The subsequent creation story found in Genesis 2:4b–2:25 is notable for its earthy language and anthropocentric (or human-centered) viewpoint. God is here portrayed not only as much less transcendent, but even as less omniscient in that humans can surprise God at times. Scholars attribute this seemingly more fallible image of God to the J source. In this account the creation of animals appears to result from a trial and error attempt to find a suitable partner for the first human being. Discovering that none of the animals would serve as a helper to Adam, God removes a piece of Adam and builds a woman whom the earth creature recognizes as his partner. Here the Torah, in a brief aside, provides the reader with an etiological, or causal, explanation of the attraction to the opposite sex and the central role of the nuclear family. Furthermore, it seems likely that the ancient author views heterosexuality to be normative in that it reaches back to the original creation of human beings. Thus the interpretation of this verse inevitably comes into play in the current heated cultural and religious debates surrounding same-sex marriage.

As one can see, these first two chapters of Genesis provide a feast of ideas. Yet one should not overlook two foundational concepts exhibited within Genesis 1–2. The first is that the Torah rarely engages in abstract analysis such as one finds in Greek philosophy or in later Christian theology. Rather, the Hebrew Bible tends to communicate its message through narratives, and these stories are open to many different readings. The result is that all readers must become interpreters and, in a sense, theologians. The second insight is connected to the placing side by side of two different, and at times even contradictory, creation stories. One of the most interesting features of the Torah is that it incorporates diverse and at times even seemingly contradictory ideas in close proximity to each other. The Hebrew Bible in general and the Torah in particular might be thought of as a lively argument spanning centuries, containing both testimonies and counter-testimonies. Such ways of presenting things have undoubtedly inspired later readers to continue to argue with the text and each other over the meaning of the Torah.

Corruption: Genesis 3–11

For centuries, Christians have read Genesis 3 as the story of the 'Fall of Man' in which God punishes all humans on account of Adam and Eve's disobedience by taking away the immortality he had initially bestowed upon them. This interpretation gave rise to the Christian doctrine of original sin, the idea that all humans are sinful at birth as a result of the first humans' actions. However, an examination of Genesis 3–11 points to a series of linked narratives that describe the ongoing corruption of human beings and God's attempts to remedy this situation. There is little evidence to suggest that Genesis 3 marks a complete change in the human–divine relationship. Furthermore, it is not clear that Genesis 3 describes a loss of human immortality, but rather the loss of the potential to obtain it. We would suggest, along with others, that Genesis 1–11 contains many interconnected stories that describe a 'falling out' between God and humans through the deepening corruption of human beings.

None of this is to argue that Genesis 3 is not significant. It is. The story reveals psychologically sophisticated and mythically compelling insights about how humans are led to sin and the ways in which sin distorts human relationships as well as fractures the three-way relationship between humanity, nature, and God. An often-missed element of this text is that it appears to contain a subtle two-pronged critique of the Deity, less surprising once one remembers that Genesis regularly portrays God as developing alongside his human creation. The first element of this implicit divine critique is that God seemed not to have anticipated how quickly humans would push beyond the limits God set, or that the snake that was created by God (possibly representing the natural world and its temptations) would be the catalyst of human corruption. The second element is that the punishments contained in this chapter at times seem disproportionately harsh. Thus all humans from this point forward suffer the consequences of this one act of disobedience. At the same time, however, we also learn that God lessens his initial threatened punishment (to kill humans for eating the forbidden fruit), thereby introducing an element of grace into the divine–human relationship.

Genesis 4 deepens the Torah's probing of human corruption by narrating the first murder, a fratricide inspired by jealousy over God's preference for Abel and his sacrifice over Cain and his. This short episode is the first of a host of stories in Genesis in which God's favor toward a specific person sets off the jealousy of those not chosen (a theme we return to below). After this incident the chapter goes on to describe a number of technological innovations, which it places between Cain's murder of Abel and Lamech's vengeful taunt. Here two particular trends stand out. Firstly, the growing ability of humans to manipulate and master the natural world is a mixed blessing in that such technical knowledge is paired with the growing corruption of human beings. We might say that for the ancient storyteller, the evolving technical mastery exhibited by humans is tainted by a lack of human moral development. The second related trend concerns the linkage between the deterioration of God's creation and the failure of human beings to occupy their proper place in the cosmos. This occurs when humans seek to become godlike as Eve and Adam attempt to do in Genesis 3, or when humans devolve into animals who engage in unrestrained violence, as witnessed in Lamech's taunt found in 4:23–4. It can also occur through threats from the divine realm, as happens in Genesis 6:1–4. Here divine beings lust after and procreate with human women, an incident that immediately precedes God's decision to destroy his creation by flood. The idea that humans who violate their place in the cosmic order jeopardize the stability of God's creation recurs in the Tower of Babel incident found in Genesis 11.

MONOTHEISM OR MONOLATRY?

The Israelites are often credited with inventing the idea of monotheism, that is, the belief that there is only one God. Further, it is often presumed that the Hebrew Bible is monotheistic throughout. However, evidence suggests that while certain later texts such as Isaiah 40–66 contain something approaching what we today might call monotheism, much of the rest of the Hebrew Bible can better be described as endorsing monolatry. The term monolatry recognizes that although multiple divine forces may exist, Israel is permitted to worship only one specific deity. Genesis itself contains several passages that suggest a plurality of divine beings, but generally speaking they are seen as subordinate to the one supreme God of the Hebrew Bible. Thus scholars would explain the plural usages found in Genesis 1:26 ('Let us make humans') and 11:7 ('Come, let us go down') as God speaking to other divine beings who function as part of his courtly retinue. It is these divine beings, literally called 'the sons of God' who mate with human women in Genesis 6:2. These beings often function as agents who work for God, and thus are sometimes called divine messengers or what we call angels. This is exactly the English term used to describe the two divine beings who are sent to rescue Lot and punish the residents of Sodom in Genesis 19:1.

When one examines the flood narrative, one once again discovers the juxtaposition of substantially differing theologies. One strand of the narrative (P) views the flood as God's righteous judgment on a wicked humanity as seen in Genesis 6:11. In contrast, the other version of the story (J) shows a more reluctant and ambivalent deity. This deity initially exhibits regret at having created humankind and at the end of the flood regrets having destroyed the world by the flood. Although the story can lend itself to the idea of an unmerciful God who destroys all at will, one can just as easily read the text as suggesting that the world only exists due to God's continuing mercy toward a humanity that remains corrupt (compare Genesis 6:5–7 with 8:21).

God is once more seen to adapt to changing circumstances when he adjusts the human diet. Originally in Genesis 1:29–30, God only permitted humans to eat vegetation, but now in Genesis 9 he allows humans to consume animal meat as long as the blood is drained prior to its consumption. This may be an implicit recognition that God's original standard which limited human and animal consumption to a vegetarian diet was unrealistic and rather than reducing violence it led to its escalation. God appears to permit the use of controlled violence by allowing the consumption of animal meat and use of capital punishment in hopes of reducing the most problematic form of human violence, murder (that is, the unwarranted taking of innocent life). This shift suggests that God is becoming ever more willing to work with humans as they are rather than as he had hoped they might be.

This passage is immediately followed by the Bible's first covenant in which God promises all humanity and all animals that he will never again flood the world. From this, traditional Judaism derives what it calls the Noahide laws, a short list of basic commandments such as not murdering, not stealing, and not committing adultery that apply to all humans, since in the biblical view everyone is a descendant of Noah. In spite of God's attempt to reduce human violence and set the human–divine relationship on a new footing, Ham's behavior toward Noah in the immediate aftermath of the flood, as well as the Babel story in Genesis 11, indicate that God is still failing to obtain the response for which he had hoped.

God and Abraham: Genesis 12–25

As already mentioned, in some ways Genesis 1–11 represents not only human failure but also God's failed attempt to create a proper set of relationships between humans, nature, and himself. In the wake of these failures, many suggest that God moves from a plan in which he demands equal obedience from all humans to a two-tiered plan in which most people are held to a minimal religio-moral standard (the few basic Noahide laws) while one man's family is given a special place in the divine economy requiring that they maintain a higher religio-moral standard (the full teachings of the Torah). As the following passage from Genesis 12:2–3 makes clear, God's special favor toward Abraham, as well as Israel, Abraham's descendants, is closely bound up with God's larger plan to bring blessing to the whole world, as God assures Abraham:

> I will make of you a great nation, and I will bless you, and make your name great, so that you will be a blessing. I will bless those who bless you, and the one who curses you I will curse; and in you all the families of the earth shall be blessed.

There is some debate regarding whether the conclusion of Genesis 12:3 should be translated as, 'In you all the families of the earth shall be blessed', or as, 'In you all the families of the earth shall bless themselves'. This is because the Hebrew word *nivrechu*, used to describe how the non-abrahamic nations of the world will experience this blessing, can be understood in more than one way. Will Abraham and his later descendants, the Israelites, mediate God's blessings to the other nations of the world through their actions? Or will the nations bless themselves through Abraham in some way, perhaps by blessing him or perhaps by saying, 'May you be blessed like God blessed Abraham'? The Hebrew is open to either reading but how one reads this word can significantly affect one's understanding of Israel's purpose and mission in the world (something we discuss below). Whatever the case, it *is* clear that according to Genesis, God's blessing of the world is mediated through Abraham and his covenantal children (Israel). At least at times, Abraham is active in this process, as attested to in the story of Sodom and Gomorrah in Genesis 18. There Abraham bargains with God in hopes of saving the people who live in these sinful cities.

The call of Abraham also includes God's gift of land to Abraham and his descendants (identified as the land of Canaan), the giving of which is instrumental to the rest of the Torah and Hebrew Bible, and central to post-biblical Jewish thought. This initial mention of land in Genesis 12:7 becomes a promise that reverberates throughout Genesis. Such an idea is undoubtedly a difficult one for the modern world, especially in the light of today's fragile Middle East. Nevertheless, it is important to note that while many contemporary readers may be uncomfortable with the idea that God gave a particular piece of land to Abraham's descendants through Isaac and Jacob, the gift of the land can be seen as an expression of God's willingness to be present in the world in which humans live. In fact, the incarnational ideas so prevalent in Christianity grew out of and only make sense in relation to the theology of the land and the temple that stood in Jerusalem for nearly 1000 years.

We briefly mentioned the topic of covenant above regarding Noah, but its central place in the Abraham narrative makes this an appropriate place to look at this important concept in more depth. A covenant is a way to formalize an agreement between two parties, and it sometimes involves a ritual element or a type of sacrifice (note that in Hebrew generally one does not *make* a covenant but rather 'cuts' [*karat*] one, likely pointing to the ritual element of slaughtering an animal in sealing the agreement). There are two broad categories of divine–human covenants in the Hebrew Bible: conditional covenants in which the bulk of the burden falls on the humans involved, and unconditional covenants in which most of the obligations fall upon God.

Genesis includes two main covenants, one between God and Noah, discussed above, and one between God and Abraham, found in Genesis 15 and 17. Both of these are unconditional covenants in that the obligations fall primarily, if not exclusively, upon the Deity. God's covenant with Abraham is a commitment to give Abraham numerous descendants as well as the land of Canaan as an everlasting possession. According to Genesis 17 and 18, Abraham's responsibility (and thus his descendants' as well) is to circumcise all male children (an act that came to be synonymous with affirming this covenant), to walk blamelessly before God, and to teach one's children likewise to 'keep the way of the LORD by doing righteousness and justice'. The fact that this covenant is given in two places, each with a different ritual (the first in Genesis 15 with the slaughter of various animals; the second in Genesis 17 with male circumcision), likely attests to two different traditions being preserved side by side.

Chosenness, strife, and reconciliation in Genesis

The remainder of Genesis is largely a saga involving three generations of one family. The first generational story rotates around two major themes, that of Abraham and Sarah's inability to have children and (later) who, of Abraham's two sons, will carry on God's covenantal relationship with Abraham. Here one finds that major tensions erupt between Hagar and Sarah, tensions that in the end lead to Hagar and Ishmael's expulsion from Abraham's household.

The second set of stories takes place in two households between two rival sets of siblings whose destinies become intertwined. It begins in the household of Isaac and Rebekah, the matriarch who bears the twins Esau and Jacob. After obtaining Esau's birthright and blessing by questionable means, Jacob, for fear of death, is forced to flee to his uncle's home in Mesopotamia. It is in Laban's household that Jacob becomes entangled in the rivalry between two sisters, Leah and Rachel, both of whom he ends up marrying. Both women (and their maidservants Bilhah and Zilpah) bear a total of twelve sons to Jacob, who become the forefathers of the twelve tribes of Israel. After tensions arise between Jacob and his father-in-law Laban, Jacob, along with his now large family, returns home to face Esau. A story of partial reconciliation occurs and then the third family saga begins in Genesis 37, which runs though the end of Genesis.

This final story concerning Jacob's sons – often called the Joseph story – is driven by the theme of both Jacob's and God's favor toward Joseph and the deep jealousy it evokes in Jacob's older ten sons. The ten brothers sell Joseph into slavery and he is taken to Egypt. Through a series of dramatic and wondrous events Joseph becomes vizier (the highest official in Egypt under the Pharaoh) and he has the chance to test his brothers when they come to buy grain in Egypt. In some sense, Benjamin, Jacob's youngest son and Joseph's only full-blooded brother, serves as the means by which the reconciliation takes place between Joseph and his ten estranged brothers. By the end of Genesis Jacob and his whole family are living as well-treated guests in Egypt.

As one can see, the themes of chosenness and the strife it engenders play a central role in the Ancestral Narratives. As noted earlier in this chapter, the idea of God's special favor toward some that in turn sparks conflict between the chosen and the non-chosen first appears in the Cain and Abel narrative in rather terse form. The same themes keep recurring in ever more developed and complex forms in the three family stories that occupy Genesis 12–50. For example, let us look at just the question of reconciliation, a theme that is precluded from occurring in Genesis 4 in that Cain murders Abel. In the story of Isaac and Ishmael there is a single verse, Genesis 25:9, that hints at a possible late-life reconciliation between these two brothers in that they both are present to bury their father Abraham. Turning to the Jacob and Esau narrative, almost all of Genesis 32–3 is taken up with the question of whether and to what extent Jacob and Esau can reconcile. In the Joseph story, this theme comes to occupy all of Genesis 42–5 as well as Genesis 50 and it stands at the center of the whole Joseph story.

We can also look a bit more deeply at the theme of special divine favor that tends to create strife as well as blessing within many of the narratives of Genesis. These Genesis stories of family rivalry highlight the idea that a younger sibling is divinely favored over the elder sibling or siblings, a motif that recurs elsewhere in the Hebrew Bible (for example, Ephraim, Moses, David, and Solomon are all favored over older siblings). The text provides little justification for God's choice, aside from the possible exception of the Cain and Abel story where interpreters have long argued over whether Cain's offering was inferior to Abel's. Yet, even there, God's enigmatic speech to Cain focuses upon Cain's reaction to God's favoritism of Abel, not the quality of Cain's offering (Genesis 4:6–7), thus highlighting the mysterious and seemingly arbitrary nature of God's choice.

This divine preference for the younger sibling suggests that God favors individuals not favored by human convention (in antiquity, typically the eldest son was favored and given a double inheritance). But why does a tradition-bound culture like ancient Israel's preserve images of a deity who does not abide by the community's norms, even those enshrined within its divinely ordained laws (for an example, see Deuteronomy 21:15–17)? One explanation for this unusual state of affairs is that the Hebrew Bible time and again reveals God's power by showing how human attempts to control outcomes are subverted by God. This recurring literary pattern might be labeled the Bible's 'underdog motif'. God's plan always prevails, frequently even by means of resistance to it or through those who seem to be marginal and powerless.

Another likely factor contributing to this motif's prominence is Israel's self-perception in relation to its older and more dominant neighbors, Egypt and Mesopotamia. While we today think of the Israelites as an archaic culture, Israel saw herself as a younger upstart who arrived on the scene long after cultures like those found in Mesopotamia and Egypt. In fact, various biblical thinkers regularly reacted against certain Mesopotamian and Egyptian religious ideas (for example, while the sun, moon, and stars were worshiped throughout the Near East, Genesis 1:14–19 describes them as simply part of nature and places them on the fourth day of creation). At least part of the reason that these stories highlight the notion that younger siblings supersede their elders by divine choice derives from Israel's own sense of her late-born status.

It is important to point out that within these narratives of sibling rivalry, the non-favored are not necessarily hated by God or excluded from God's blessing. When one looks at the language in Genesis 17 and 21 describing Ishmael's status, it is clear that even though he is outside the covenant, he is just barely outside it. Not only is Ishmael circumcised, thereby receiving the bodily mark of the very covenant from which he is excluded, but he receives a special divine blessing. Much the same can be said of Esau who prospers in life and fathers a host of progeny (Genesis 36). In fact, even Cain was not driven from God because he was not chosen, but rather because his jealousy drove him to kill his favored sibling. Chosenness is not to be equated with a guarantee of salvation, and non-chosenness is not a sign of damnation.

It is also clear that being chosen is not a purely positive experience. Chosenness often brings mortal danger in its wake. Thus Abel is killed; Abraham is driven by famine to Egypt where his life is in potential danger; Isaac is nearly sacrificed to God by Abraham; Jacob was in danger of being murdered by his brother Esau; and Joseph is nearly killed by his brothers. This pattern of the endangerment of the chosen, which usually precedes the eventual triumph or exaltation of the divinely favored one, is central to both the Hebrew Bible and the New Testament, as indicated by the Exodus and Gospel narratives. Thus both the master story of Israel, which is the account of the Egyptian enslavement and eventual freeing of Israel from this bondage found in Exodus 1–15, and the Gospel Passion narratives, which describe the death and resurrection of Jesus, are intensifications of the major theme of Genesis. In short, both Jews and Christians see themselves as God's favored child, who experiences a tribulation that may result in death, but who ultimately triumphs and is symbolically or actually resurrected into a new life provided by the grace of God.

Examples of Jewish use of Genesis

The book of Genesis has left its mark on later Jewish religious thought in a host of ways. To begin, the creation narratives gave rise to a good deal of Jewish mystical and philosophical speculation spanning across many centuries. Aside from this, Jewish legal and moral tradition has often probed the characters in Genesis and their actions, including the character of God and his actions, to derive legal and behavioral norms. For example, as noted in chapter 2, the Rabbis highlighted the importance of clothing the naked by noting that the first action God does for Adam and Eve after they eat the fruit from the forbidden tree (the specific fruit is not named in the Bible) is to provide them with garments (Genesis 3:21). Frequently Jewish tradition compares characters to draw contrasting moral portraits. Thus Noah is contrasted negatively with Abraham because Noah raised no objection to God's plan to flood the world due to human evils, while Abraham engaged in a spirited set of arguments to prevent God from destroying the cities of Sodom and Gomorrah too hastily. Ultimately Abraham convinced God that if there were ten righteous individuals in these two cities, all their inhabitants, including the many wicked ones, would be spared. Interestingly enough, some streams of Jewish tradition link the rule that one needs a minimum of ten adult congregants (according to orthodox Judaism ten males over thirteen years of age) for a prayer quorum (in Hebrew a *minyan*) to this story, in that Abraham saw ten as the minimum number for a viable community.

Unsurprisingly, Jewish tradition developed a vast array of post-biblical stories that fill out the lives of the Patriarchs and Matriarchs. Here we will give but one short example in which the ancient Rabbis provide background information that explains why God eventually chose Abraham as the founder of the Israelite people. This is taken from an early midrash collection focused on Genesis, called *Genesis Rabbah*. In this passage, Abraham is presented as someone who openly rejected the idol-based religion of his father by realizing that idol worship was foolish.

Terah [Abraham's father] was a manufacturer of idols. He once went away somewhere and left Abraham to sell them [the idols] in his place ... [Once] a woman came with a plateful of flour and requested of him, 'Take this and offer it to them.' So he took a stick, broke them, and put the stick in the hand of the largest. When his father returned he demanded, 'What have you done to them?' 'I cannot conceal it from you,' he [Abraham] rejoined. 'A woman came with a plateful of fine meal and requested me to offer it to them. One claimed, "I must eat first", while another claimed, "I must eat first." Thereupon the largest arose, took the stick, and broke them.' 'Why do you mock me,' he [Terah] cried out; 'have they any knowledge!' 'Should not your ears listen to what your mouth is saying,' he [Abraham] retorted.

(*Genesis Rabbah*, 38.13, Soncino translation)

One of the largest imprints left upon Jewish tradition by Genesis is found in the way that the story of Abraham's near sacrifice of Isaac, what Jewish tradition calls the *akedah* (or *binding*) of Isaac, has affected the daily and yearly liturgical cycle. This story is recited during the preliminary prayers of the daily morning service. Furthermore, the *akedah* is the Torah portion read on the second day of Rosh Hashanah, the Jewish New Year festival that occurs each fall. In Jewish tradition, Rosh Hashanah is the time when God takes stock of all human lives and determines one's destiny for the next year. The reading of this Torah text on Rosh Hashanah suggests that all Jews recognize that God has a claim on their lives that he could choose to exercise anytime. If one is given another year to live, this is an act of pure divine grace, like God's provision of the ram caught in the thicket that provided a substitute for the life of Isaac in Genesis 22. Thus the community as a whole as well as the individuals who compose the community see themselves as only continuing to exist by an ongoing act of divine grace.

Examples of Christian use of Genesis

The importance of Genesis to the New Testament and Christianity is indeed great. Naturally, Jesus (as a Jew) and the early Church (initially as a Jewish sect) would have assumed Genesis as a foundation for their thought, ranging in ideas from God as creator of the world, the value of all human life,

Adam and Abraham as the primary ancestors of humanity and Israel, to God's election of Israel. It is also clear that Genesis played an important role in the teachings of Jesus, and at times Jesus would use Genesis as a 'trump card' in debates about the law or particulars of religious life. For example, as we mentioned in chapter 2, when the Pharisees test Jesus regarding whether divorce is permissible, they mention that Moses (that is, the Torah) permitted a certificate of divorce according to Deuteronomy 24:1–4. In this case, Jesus decides to counter them by appealing not to a specific Torah commandment, but to the creation story of Genesis, arguing that 'from the beginning' a man and woman become 'one flesh' in marriage, not to be separated again.

However, probably more than any other passage in Genesis – indeed the Torah or even Hebrew Bible – the Call of Abraham in Genesis 12:1–3 stands at the center of Christian theological reflection. While there is little doubt that the passage is of utmost importance for Judaism as well, here the issues become murky in that each tradition tends to emphasize different aspects of the passage and, further, the above-mentioned translational difficulty in 12:3 plays a pivotal role in each tradition's self-understanding.

Christian theology has built much upon Genesis 12:1–3 in that many Christians see here the foundations of mission and God's bringing of salvation to the larger world (for both Jew and Gentile). There is little debate that the Jewishness of Jesus is important to Christian theology, and it is important precisely because he is a descendant of Abraham, and eventually David – the one through whom the messiah is said to come (that Matthew's gospel begins with a genealogy, mentioning Jesus' lineage to both figures, is not insignificant). The thinking in Christianity is that God will bless the entire world through Abraham as stated in Genesis 12:3. As discussed in chapter 2, Jesus is seen as the seed of Abraham who would mediate God's blessing toward Abraham to the larger world. The apostle Paul underlines this point in his reading of Genesis 15:6, where Abraham is said to believe in this promise of God. Paul argues that through his belief (and *not* through keeping the law), Abraham is said to attain righteousness, or salvation. Paul then goes on to explain that *Genesis 12:3 is itself the very gospel*, or good news, by drawing an analogy between Abraham's belief and the belief of those who recognize that Jesus is the Christ (a Greek word meaning the anointed one, or messiah):

> Just as Abraham 'believed God, and it was reckoned to him as righteousness', so, you see, those who believe are the descendants of Abraham. And the scripture, foreseeing that God would justify the Gentiles by faith, declared the gospel beforehand to Abraham, saying, 'All the Gentiles shall be blessed in you.' For this reason, those who believe are blessed with Abraham who believed.
>
> (Galatians 3:6–9)

There is much that could be said, but our purpose here is not to evaluate the relative persuasiveness of Paul's argument. Our point is, rather, to show how texts drawn from Genesis have been used in both the Jewish and Christian traditions. The relationship of faith and works to salvation as drawn from this passage is certainly a matter of debate, something a comparison of Galatians 3:1–14 and James 2:14–26 readily reveals. Such a comparison also reveals that the compilers of the New Testament show continuity with the Torah by once more affirming that the biblical tradition is broad enough to contain texts that stand in tension with each other.

Conclusion

The book of Genesis and its stories of creation, Noah, and Abraham have exerted extraordinary influence over Western culture for over two thousand years and they continue to do so today. Attempts to reshape the socio-political order of the West have time and again involved disputes that invoke the Bible more generally, with certain passages from Genesis often receiving a good deal of attention. One could argue that the ongoing movement toward greater inclusion of once marginalized voices is an attempt to realize Genesis' insight that all humans are worthy of some fundamental dignity because we are all created in God's image. Thus one should not be surprised that Genesis played an important part in the debates over slavery and women's rights, and that it continues to be a touchstone in current discussions surrounding the treatment of the environment, the acceptance or rejection of homosexuality, and more broadly on issues surrounding family values.

In short, studying Genesis is far from an exercise relevant only to historians interested in ancient Israelite culture or to theologians seeking to ground various doctrines in the biblical text. Genesis is not only the first biblical book in literary sequence, it is as well the book that contains the foundation for biblical teachings on the character of God, the root causes of human sin, and ultimately what it means to be human – created in God's own image yet dwelling on earth.

5

Exodus

Introduction and placement in the Torah

The second book in the Torah is called Exodus in English, a reference to the book's central narrative about God's redemption of the Israelites from Egyptian enslavement. While the English title follows the traditional Greek and Latin designations, Jews refer to this book as *Shemoth*, meaning 'Names' (short for 'And these are the names'), from the opening Hebrew words of Exodus 1:1 that introduce the names of the sons of Jacob who journeyed down to Egypt.

Exodus is the second longest book in the Torah, just ahead of Numbers, containing some 1209 verses distributed over 40 chapters. The placement of Exodus in the Pentateuch may not seem to be of particular importance until we come to appreciate that the story would make little sense apart from the Genesis material. Genesis sets the stage in important ways, not least in explaining the origins of the people Israel and why Israel is in Egypt. Largely unexplained concepts in Exodus – such as the importance of Israel having become a numerous people, the LORD's ownership of that people, traveling to a 'Promised Land', or even the LORD's resolve to remain with Israel despite being a rebellious people – are all intricately related to events in the previous book. Further, as mentioned in our discussion of Genesis, it is important to recognize that the Torah begins not with Israel or with the commandments of the Torah, but with all humanity and the creation of the larger, universal, world. It is in Exodus that the narrowed focus which began in Genesis 12 becomes fully assumed and continues throughout the rest of the Hebrew Bible.

Exodus also leads quite naturally into Leviticus. The instructions given in Leviticus assume the existence of the newly constructed tabernacle, the completion of which is described in the last chapter of Exodus. Exodus closes with God's glory descending into the tabernacle and Leviticus continues from this point, explicating how Israel is to live in God's presence.

Overview of Exodus

Exodus is relatively easy to outline. Exodus 1–15 contains the story of the Egyptian oppression of the Israelites, which leads into the Ten Plagues and culminates in the crossing of the Sea of Reeds (traditionally but likely incorrectly rendered as the Red Sea) by the Israelites, and the drowning of the pursuing Egyptian army. Exodus 16–18 contains several narratives dealing with Israel's journey to Mount Sinai. Chapters 19–24 relate the story of the encounter between God and the Israelites at Mount Sinai, which includes the giving of the Ten Commandments as well as a host of other legislation. Chapters 25–31 and 35–40 contain detailed instructions on building and consecrating the portable tent-shrine that the Israelites travel with on their wanderings toward the Holy Land. In the middle of this material one finds the Golden Calf episode and a reaffirmation of God's relationship to Israel in the wake of this breach.

Contemporary controversies

Scholars have long argued over the extent to which Exodus grows out of memories of actual historical events. The current consensus is that the general portrayal of a united Israelite people going down to Egypt, multiplying, being enslaved and being freed en masse, is based on a national legend popular during the monarchic period that attempts to narrate Israel's understanding of her national origins and the meaning of her peoplehood. However, many scholars still believe that at least some ancestors of the ancient Israelites may have escaped Egyptian bondage and that the book contains a number of details that illuminate aspects of the origins of Israel's religion. Thus the role played by Jethro, Moses' Midianite father-in-law, is often understood to provide an important clue about ancient Israel's attachment to a God who appeared at a mountain in the Sinai Peninsula near Midian. Further, Israel's monotheistic impulses are sometimes traced back to a specific period in Egyptian religious history on the basis of the prominence of Moses, a character who is raised in Pharaoh's palace. Perhaps the most useful way to think of the narratives in Exodus is as a blend of myth and history by which Israel expressed her historical origins in mythic terms, a point that will be discussed in greater detail in relation to the splitting of the Sea of Reeds.

Two related issues tend to animate a good deal of historical scholarship on the book of Exodus. The first is the *date* of the migration from Egypt (and the eventual 'conquest' of Canaan) and the second is the *route* that the people took in traveling to Canaan. Depending on one's stance toward the historical reliability of the book (that is, how much 'actually happened' and how much is better characterized as mythic in nature), scholars will spend extensive, little, or no time discussing such questions. The issues are complicated for a number of reasons, not least because the book itself is generally uninterested in these questions and it gives little by way of detail to assist the scholar in this task (for example, the names of the Pharaohs in Egypt are not given and neither is the precise location at which Israel crosses the ambiguously named 'Sea of Reeds').

Moses and Israel in Egypt: Exodus 1–6

Let us now examine the book in more detail and draw out some of its major emphases. In language evocative of both Genesis 1 and Genesis 50, Exodus opens with a note on how the meager group of seventy Israelites who journeyed down to Egypt had abundantly multiplied and how a new Pharaoh who did not know Joseph was threatened by Israel's fertility. This Pharaoh's initial plan was to impose harsh servitude on the one-time guest Israelites. But Exodus 1:15–22 narrates a brief attempt at ethnic genocide when Pharaoh commands the midwives who attend to the Israelites to kill every male Israelite immediately upon delivery. The midwives, fearing God, ignore Pharaoh's orders and lie to his face. In turn, God rewards them.

There are many interpretive issues raised by this terse and compelling story that narrates how the first act of resistance to the most powerful human on earth came from two lowly midwives. In particular, there is the question of the nationality of the midwives (discussed in 'Hebrew matters' below) and the variant ways in which this story was received by Jews and Christians. Regarding the latter, it is interesting to note that the story itself seems completely unashamed of the fact that the midwives lie. Here one sees a major split between some of the most important streams of Christian versus Jewish understandings of this story. In general, classical Jewish interpreters have not been troubled by the fact that the midwives lied because in rabbinic Judaism one may not only suspend certain religious behaviors to save a life but in special circumstances one may be commanded to invert certain rules. Thus, among traditional Jews one may not drive a car on the Sabbath, but if a life is in danger and driving is necessary, one *must* drive on Sabbath. Since the midwives were saving lives, Jewish interpreters see no problem with the behavior of the midwives. One finds a substantially different view in the work of St Augustine called *Against Lying* in which he argues that although the midwives are to be praised for sparing Israelite babies, they are to be criticized for lying to Pharaoh. Augustine acknowledges that if they told the truth they may well have been killed, but he asserts that having been killed, and in some sense martyred, they would have received a heavenly reward greater than the earthly reward the text describes God giving them in verse 21. The point here is not to resolve this interpretive difficulty by endorsing one view as correct, but to demonstrate how small details are used to bolster the larger theological claims of each faith community.

HEBREW MATTERS: WERE THE MIDWIVES ISRAELITE OR EGYPTIAN?

In most English translations of Exodus it is clearly stated that the midwives were Hebrews. The difficulty here, however, is twofold. One involves the question of whether the rest of the story supports the notion that these women were in fact Israelites. And here the evidence is split. While their names sound Semitic rather than Egyptian, the fact that they are said to 'fear God' and that Pharaoh expects that they will do as he says may indicate they are Egyptian employees of Pharaoh. After all, Joseph, when he is still hiding behind his Egyptian identity in Genesis 42, uses almost identical language, stating that he will test the words of his brothers because ultimately he 'fears God'. Furthermore, most translations of the Hebrew follow the Masoretic or traditional Jewish vocalization of the ancient text, a vocalization system that is much younger than the text itself. As noted in chapter 1, originally these texts were written with only consonants and thus if one views, say, the Dead Sea Scrolls one notices the complete lack of written vowels. In some instances, such as this one, a very slight vowel change affects the way one understands the relationship between two adjacent words. Therefore, it may be that the text should actually be translated as 'the midwives of the Hebrews' rather than 'the Hebrew midwives', leaving open the plausible possibility that these were Egyptian

**HEBREW MATTERS: WERE THE MIDWIVES
ISRAELITE OR EGYPTIAN?** *(cont.)*

women who served as the midwives of the Hebrew women. Such a
reading also seems to make Pharaoh more intelligent and nefarious
in his assumption that Egyptian midwives might share his hatred of
the alien Israelites. More importantly, it indicates that one need not
be a Hebrew to be a righteous human being, a point reinforced in
the very next chapter when Pharaoh's own daughter saves the life
of the Israelite baby she names Moses.

The narrative proceeds immediately to the birth of Moses
and his mother's attempt to keep the baby hidden in an effort
to preserve his life. The story draws from a common motif in
antiquity in which the hero's life is endangered but providentially
saved before he assumes his role (in fact there is a strikingly similar
story in other ancient Near Eastern literature about King Sargon
of Akkad who lived around 2350 BCE, which is about 1000 years
before Moses lived). Realizing that the boy is growing too big to
hide, Moses' mother conceives a plan to place him in a floating
basket on the river. Here English readers completely miss the
fact that a rather unusual Hebrew word (*tevah*) is used for Moses'
basket, the same word used of Noah's ark, thus drawing a parallel
between these two stories where everything floats tenuously on
the waters. As Moses' sister looks on, she witnesses the basket
being discovered by Pharaoh's own daughter. When the daughter
of Pharaoh opens the basket and hears the crying child, she takes
pity on the child even while acknowledging the Hebrew origins
of the baby. That it is Pharaoh's daughter who saves Moses
indicates that not all Egyptians are evil. Pharaoh's daughter in
turn ends up hiring Moses' mother to nurse baby Moses, creating
an irony in which Pharaoh is providing extensive support to raise

the very person who will eventually free the Israelite slaves and bring ruin on Egypt in the process.

While we never learn exactly how Moses discovered his Israelite roots, the story jumps forward in time to narrate Moses' first attempt to intercede on behalf of an oppressed Israelite by killing an Egyptian taskmaster. The text makes no judgment on the morality of this act, but does imply that such solo interventions are ultimately ineffective in that Moses is soon forced to flee Egypt. He escapes into Midianite territory where he comes to the defense of seven women shepherds who are the daughters of a Midianite priest, and ends up marrying one of them.

At this point the text introduces God more explicitly into the process that will eventually lead Pharaoh to free the Israelite slaves by noting that Israel's oppression-induced cries had grabbed God's attention. This is a parade example of the way in which ancient Israel understood God as a personality who can be affected by humans. Israel's groaning under Egyptian bondage causes the Deity to remember his covenantal promises to Israel's Patriarchs. And so God appears to Moses in the Burning Bush, an encounter that occupies one and a half chapters of Exodus. Many readers are surprised to learn not only the length of this interlude, but also its unusual content. It consists of an extended dialogue between a flexible God and a very reluctant Moses in which God tolerates Moses' complaints until God eventually compromises by letting Aaron assist Moses. This sets the stage for the coming dramatic contest between God and Pharaoh.

A number of aspects of this lengthy encounter are worth highlighting. In addition to the revelation of the Tetragrammaton, YHWH, God's personal name, perhaps most startling to modern readers is that God is portrayed as neither fully omniscient nor entirely unchanging. Rather, God's character is first and foremost relational, defined in relation to Israel (he is the same God who appeared to Israel's ancestors) and to his being (the enigmatic phrase in Exodus 3:14 is often translated 'I AM WHO I AM').

This rather non-traditional view of God – a God who is not all-knowing or immutable – is seen immediately in Exodus 4 when God gives Moses a number of miraculous signs to perform in hopes of convincing the Israelites that he was indeed sent by God to begin the process of their redemption. God explicitly tells Moses that he is not sure if the first or second sign will ultimately 'do the trick' or if he will need to use yet a third sign. Exodus 4 leaves one with the distinct impression that a flexible and responsive God only reluctantly added Aaron into the plan as an assistant to Moses in order to persuade Moses to agree to his request. Once more we see that God works with humans as they are to move human history forward.

While the Israelites are quickly convinced that God has spoken to Moses, Moses and Aaron are much less effective in convincing Pharaoh. Of course, this ineffectiveness is useful to build narrative tension and the narrator of the story gives it theological meaning by telling the reader in advance that Pharaoh's stubbornness will allow God to demonstrate his miraculous control of nature (Exodus 3:19–22). But this also allows the story to mirror the ways in which revolutionary changes often occur. In particular, it is quite common when powerful forces are challenged for those forces to become more implacable and for them to increase their oppressive grip on those they hold in thrall. One only needs to think of the American civil rights struggle in which the initial attempts to enfranchise southern African Americans led to an escalation in the oppression of those same African Americans. In Exodus 5, Moses and Aaron's initial attempt to speak to Pharaoh on behalf of the Israelites results in Pharaoh's order that the Israelites will no longer be given straw but must now gather their own straw and yet still meet the same daily quota of bricks. Pharaoh's logic, like that of certain corporations resistant to organized unions, is that if the Israelites have time to discuss their working conditions they must be slacking off their jobs and have too little to keep them occupied. Here the NRSV's translation of

5:17 as 'you are lazy, lazy' can be translated as 'you are slackers, slackers'. Furthermore, the actions of Moses and Aaron fractured the Israelite resistance to Pharaoh because Pharaoh ordered his taskmasters to beat the Israelite supervisors when they failed to meet their quotas. These supervisors in turn became angry with Moses and Aaron for making their bad situation even worse. Moses' lament to God following this episode shows how human prayer, even prayer born of frustration, is part of the process of redemption. Here one also has a realistic portrayal of what often occurs when individuals or groups seek to challenge the status quo. Such challenges regularly result in initially making the situation of the oppressed worse than it was.

The plagues: Exodus 7–15

The bulk of chapters 7–15 is taken up with the sequence of escalating plagues. It is worth noting that because of certain peculiarities and repetitions in the plagues, almost all critics believe that the current plague narrative combines several sources, each of which had fewer plagues in them. This can be easily seen by the fact that the fifth plague describes the total destruction of Egyptian livestock but one finds livestock alive and well in subsequent plagues, ready to be destroyed again (see Exodus 9:6; 9:10; 9:25; and 11:5). It is possible that the variant portrayals of exactly how Pharaoh's heart (or will) is hardened with each plague also ultimately stems from the fact that Exodus is a composite narrative:

Plague 1.   'Pharaoh's heart stiffened' (Exodus 7:22)
Plague 2.   'He [Pharaoh] hardened his heart' (Exodus 8:15)
Plague 3.   'Pharaoh's heart stiffened' (Exodus 8:19)
Plague 4.   'Pharaoh hardened his heart' (Exodus 8:32)
Plague 5.   'the heart of Pharaoh hardened' (Exodus 9:7)

Plague 6.   'the LORD stiffened Pharaoh's heart' (Exodus 9:12)
Plague 7.   'he sinned once more and hardened his heart' (Exodus 9:34) followed by 'Pharaoh's heart stiffened' (Exodus 9:35)
Plague 8.   'the LORD stiffened Pharaoh's heart' (Exodus 10:20)
Plague 9.   'the LORD stiffened Pharaoh's heart' (Exodus 10:27)
Plague 10. (before crossing the Sea of Reeds) 'the LORD stiffened Pharaoh's heart' (Exodus 14:8)

There are two different Hebrew words being used here (translated 'hardened' and 'stiffened') with two different subjects, thus creating four distinct descriptions of Pharaoh's implacability. It may be that variant sources spoke of God's control of events using different language because each source had a unique view regarding the balance between God's providential control of events and the ability of humans to affect a particular situation.

However, it is possible to give a holistic literary reading to the current form of the text. In fact, some scholars challenge the suggestion of a composite text (at least with regard to the hardening of Pharaoh's heart) in that there does seem to be a balanced symmetry in the verbs used to describe the hardening of Pharaoh's will; of the twenty occurrences of the verbs used, ten have God as subject, and ten have Pharaoh (or his heart) as subject. In such a holistic reading one might emphasize that early on Pharaoh had more control over events but, as is common with, say, addictive personalities, at a certain point one loses control over one's ability to resist certain patterns of action. The text could be read as signaling a gradual reduction in Pharaoh's ability to act freely as God's control grows ever greater over the course of the unfolding narrative.

Similarly, while the multiplication of plagues may stem from the text's composite character, one can see progressions in the narrative as a whole. Thus the series of plagues arises out of God's wish to demonstrate to Pharaoh that God's claim on the

Israelites supersedes Pharaoh's. Here one must remember that the Egyptian Pharaoh was considered to be a divine being, and it is precisely this claim that the Exodus story tests. In fact, one might usefully understand the plague sequence as a contest – perhaps a showdown of sorts – between two personalities, each of whom claims to be God. The God of the Hebrew Bible triumphs in this story by demonstrating that he, *not* Pharaoh, is the God who created and controls the universe.

Broadly speaking, the sequence of plagues mirrors the order of creation. Thus the first two plagues, turning the Nile to blood and the plague of frogs, both indicate God's control over the waters. The next several plagues deal with God's control over land, the second major realm of God's creative activity in Genesis 1. While the plague of gnats in Exodus 8 involves flying creatures, they are low-level flying pests that are brought into existence when Aaron strikes the dust of the earth with his staff. The fourth plague is more difficult to fit into this category, according to the translation found in most contemporary Bibles: 'swarms of flies'. However, the Hebrew word is rare and Jewish tradition renders it as 'wild animals'. In any case, the fifth and sixth plagues, which deal with livestock and festering boils, certainly demonstrate God's control of the domain of land. Hail and locusts, plagues seven and eight, in turn demonstrate God's control of the heavens. Plague nine in which God darkens Egypt is a demonstration of God's ability to control light and darkness, an ability first used on the first day of creation. And finally, God's power to create living human beings, God's final creative act in Genesis 1, is alluded to in the tenth plague, which involves the killing of all firstborn Egyptians.

At this point in the narrative, there is a very odd but important pause. Chapters 12 and 13 contain detailed rules for the celebration of Passover. What is odd is that one would expect the first ritual re-enactment of Passover, the holiday that celebrates the Exodus from Egypt, to occur in the future, that is, after the event. But in Exodus, the very Israelites about to leave

Egypt are also the first participants celebrating the remembrance of leaving Egypt by following a prescribed ritual. (Exodus 12:48 even specifies who may partake in the Passover as if already in the land of Canaan.) Interestingly enough, later Jews who celebrate Passover read from a set liturgy that includes a command that individuals are to celebrate as if they themselves came out of Egypt *this very night*. Thus time is collapsed in both directions in this ritual in that those Israelites leaving Egypt act like later Jews celebrating Passover and later Jews celebrating Passover act as if they are ancient Israelites leaving slavery in Egypt. Furthermore, a very close analogue to this situation can be found in the origins of the Eucharist (or Holy Communion), in which Jesus self-consciously creates a ritual that he sees future Christians following. It should be noted that this ritual created by Jesus occurs at the Last Supper, a meal that several gospel writers place at Passover and which has traditionally been linked to its observance, even regarded by many Christians to replace it – Jesus himself becoming the sacrificial lamb (1 Corinthians 5:6–8).

Exodus 14 and 15 contain a prose followed by a poetic version of the crossing of the Sea of Reeds. Many scholars believe that the poetic text in Exodus 15 is one of the oldest passages (if not *the* oldest) in the Hebrew Bible. If this is correct, Exodus 14 would be a prose attempt to explain the poetic imagery of chapter 15 in a more linear fashion. One can glimpse this in the somewhat variant images found in Exodus 14. For example, Exodus 14 juxtaposes more plausible images with other more miraculous explanations. While in verses 21–5 the action is caused naturally when an east wind blows all night and leaves a muddy marsh into which the Egyptian chariots sink, in verses 26–9 the Israelites cross on dry ground with walls of water on their right and left while the Egyptians are drowned when the waters suddenly return to their normal depth. It is most likely that if Exodus 15 contains an actual historical remembrance, this remembrance is now clothed in mythic images. The particular mythic images used here are borrowed from wider Near Eastern creation mythology, which regularly depicts evil forces as chaotic waters that must be split open and subdued before creation can occur. In Exodus this theme involves not only a newly ordered world, but God's enthronement in his temple (note Exodus 15:17–18). Trying to recover a clear history from these mythic images is probably akin to trying to write a history of the War of 1812 on the basis of the Star-Spangled Banner.

On the way to Mount Sinai: Exodus 16–18

These three chapters narrate a number of incidents that occur between the Exodus event and Israel's arrival at Mount Sinai. Several of these are stories that recur in Numbers and are part of a larger tradition of Israel's murmurings against God. There is also a battle with Amalek, one of Israel's arch-enemies, followed by a long chapter in which Jethro, Moses' father-in-law, meets up with the Israelites and helps reorganize Israel's judicial system to alleviate some of Moses' burdens. It is worth observing that Exodus 18 provides a positive Israelite portrait of the status of foreigners immediately after Exodus 17's negative picture of the Amalekites. In the case of Jethro, not only is a non-Israelite viewed as acting morally, but a non-Israelite reshapes Israel's whole system of justice.

The giving of the Law: Exodus 19–24

Exodus 19–24 stands at the beginning of the very long central portion of the Torah that runs all the way from Exodus 19:1 to Numbers 10:10 dealing with Israel's time encamped at Mount Sinai. While the vast majority of the material from Genesis 1–Exodus 18 is narrative, the fact is that the Torah is in many ways primarily a law book. Therefore one should not be surprised that the story of God's revelation of his divine law to Israel features so prominently. Exodus 19 narrates Israel's arrival at the sacred mountain and the various preparations that are made for Israel's encounter with God. The chapter has many ambiguities in it, especially concerning the exact location of Moses, the Israelites, and God and some argue that these are an ingenious attempt to capture the moment of revelation from several differing angles. Such a momentous occasion would inevitably overwhelm those who experienced it, and in turn leave them with various explanations of what happened.

Exodus 20 contains the first of two recountings of the Ten Commandments, words repeated a second time in Deuteronomy 5 in a slightly modified form. It should be noted that although the term 'Ten Commandments' is not incorrect conceptually, the Hebrew text (and Jewish tradition) refers to these as the 'Ten Words' or 'Ten Principles' or 'Ten Utterances' (*aseret hadevarim*; *aseret hadibrot*). There are at least three traditions of counting the Ten Commandments with some variance between these systems. According to Jewish tradition, the first 'utterance' is not in fact a commandment but a statement, which is found in Exodus 20:2: 'I am the Lord your God, who took you out of the land of Egypt, out of the house of slavery.' The Protestant tradition understands Exodus 20:2 as a preface to the Ten Commandments and sees the first command beginning with Exodus 20:3. Other variations can be seen in figure 7.

While the Ten Commandments are specially marked out by the narrative framework of Exodus 20 and contain several laws fundamental to human society, one must not lose sight of the fact that for ancient Israel all of the laws within Exodus 20–3, and even more broadly within the larger Pentateuch, are understood to be revealed at Sinai. When one examines the array of laws in Exodus 21–3 – a collection scholars call the Covenant Code – one finds many differing categories of law. There are of course criminal laws, such as the law against kidnapping found

Commandment	Jewish	Catholic	Protestant
I am the Lord your God	I		Preface
You shall have no other gods before me	2	I	I
You shall not make for yourself an idol			2
You shall not make wrongful use of the name of God	3	2	3
Remember the Sabbath day, and keep it holy	4	3	4
Honor your father and your mother	5	4	5
You shall not murder	6	5	6
You shall not commit adultery	7	6	7
You shall not steal	8	7	8
You shall not bear false witness	9	8	9
You shall not covet your neighbor's wife	10	9	10
You shall not covet anything else of your neighbor's		10	

Figure 7 Comparison of the Ten Commandments in Judaism, Catholicism, and Protestantism

in Exodus 21:16, laws concerning civil matters such as the law about damages caused by leaving an open pit in Exodus 21:33–4, ritual laws like those concerning certain festivals discussed in Exodus 23:14–17, and even moral laws such as the command in Exodus 23:4 to return the stray ox or donkey of one's enemy. In the Israelite perspective, all human behaviors, whether primarily involving God or primarily involving one's neighbor, are behaviors God has an interest in seeing performed properly. Furthermore, God issues these commandments to the community as a whole and the whole community is held responsible for their observance. Therefore, when one wrongs one's neighbor, one also wrongs God and the larger community. Further, an offense against God is also an offense against one's neighbor that implicates the larger community.

The close link between the Exodus story and God's giving of the commandments at Sinai affects one's understanding of the narrative as a whole. Many contemporary interpreters read the Exodus event as a story about being brought from slavery into freedom. According to the story itself, however, the real issues relate to who Israel is, to whom they belong, and whom they will serve. The story describes a *change of ownership* in that it narrates Israel's movement from degrading bondage to Pharaoh, who claims to be a god but is simply an arrogant human being, to the humane serving of God who in fact has a right to claim human beings as his slaves. That the Israelites are considered 'God's slaves' is evident from passages like Leviticus 25:55, though this is often obscured because many translations render the Hebrew word for 'slaves' as 'servants'.

Finally, when God finishes giving his instruction (or Torah) to the people, Exodus 24 describes a formal concluding ritual in which Moses sprinkles the blood from certain sacrificed animals on the altar and the assembled Israelites. It is likely that this ritual is a way of symbolically representing that now Israel stands in relation to God and his commandments as a people connected by blood, people who are in effect part of the same royal family, a family with God as its fatherly monarch.

Where will God dwell? Exodus 25–31 and 35–40

Chapters 25–31 describe in detail the measurements and implements needed to construct the portable tent shrine, which the

Torah reports Israel carried through her desert wanderings, as well as the rituals needed to inaugurate the priests and the shrine. Exodus 35–40 then narrates the actual construction of this elaborately decorated and colorful shrine, which the Torah calls the Tent of Meeting. While many of these details will seem strange to contemporary Western readers, it is worth emphasizing that sacrificial worship was at one time the most common way for human communities to express their relationship to the divine, and it remains widespread in many parts of the world. Furthermore, both contemporary Jews and Christians belong to religions in which the logic of sacrifice remains central, even if the practice of actual sacrifice has been replaced by symbolic substitutes. Within Judaism, traditional Jews read the sacrificial liturgy and this functions as a symbolic substitute in place of sacrifice until such a time as the temple in Jerusalem is rebuilt and sacrifice reinstituted. Furthermore, many rituals contain sacrificial import such as circumcision or the act of fasting on certain days. Within Christianity, Jesus' death is usually understood as a type of sacrifice and the Eucharist clearly contains sacrificial overtones. Aside from this, these ancient texts make clear that humans are embodied creatures and as such we seek to worship God in ways that engage all our senses. The different types of material items (embroidered fabrics, ornately crafted wood and metal objects) and the various rituals (anointing with fragrant oil, burning incense, the sacrifice of animals) mentioned in these chapters seemed designed to stimulate the human senses on multiple levels.

Worshiping the Golden Calf: Exodus 32–4

In the middle of the Tent of Meeting instructional manual, one finds the Golden Calf episode. Occurring almost immediately after Israel encounters God directly in his proclamation of the Ten

Commandments, Israel commits what might best be described as adultery on her honeymoon night by building and worshiping an idol. This story raises a number of points worthy of emphasis. To begin, when God in anger proposes to annihilate the whole Israelite people, Moses rises to the occasion and engages in an argument with God even more audacious than that employed by Abraham in Genesis 18 (when Abraham attempted to save Sodom from God's wrath). In fact, in Exodus 32:32, despite earlier divine promises to make Moses the new patriarch and reward him greatly, Moses essentially tells God that he must forgive the Israelites for this sin or he will quit. Moses raises two arguments to support his point. Firstly, he invokes the promises God made earlier to the Patriarchs. Secondly, Moses argues that if God destroys the Israelites it will make God look capricious or even stupid in the eyes of the Egyptians from whom he had just delivered the people. Equally important is that Exodus 34 contains another telling of the commandments, which seems to indicate that God's covenantal relationship with Israel has been restored and put on new footing. But the footing is now one of total grace, because it is based on God's forgiveness of Israel after the sin of the Golden Calf. In fact, Exodus 34:6–7 contains a list of divine attributes heavily weighted toward God's loving and forgiving nature which feature prominently in the liturgy Jews recite during the High Holidays in which each Jew and the larger community seek forgiveness for their sins. Israel only stands in relationship to God because of God's willingness to abide with an imperfect people. This idea animates much of the legislation found in Leviticus, the next book in the Torah.

Examples of Jewish use of Exodus

The story of God's redemption of the Israelites and his giving of the laws at Sinai remain at the center of post-biblical Judaism.

As mentioned briefly above, the Exodus events are retold at length in every Jewish household on Passover Eve. But this is far from the only time they are mentioned. Jews recite the story of their redemption from Egypt multiple times a day in the daily prayer liturgy, and the liturgy of almost all Jewish holidays includes a reference to the Exodus experience. In fact, the manual used on Passover, the Haggadah, at one point assimilates the many tribulations experienced by Jews over thousands of years to the Exodus pattern of tribulation, which is followed by eventual divine redemption. This should not be surprising because already within the Jewish Bible itself the Exodus is regularly invoked as the prime example of God's redemptive abilities and it is seen as a harbinger of God's future redemptive activities (Psalm 106; Isaiah 43:14–21). Furthermore, the very structure of the book of Exodus, which closely ties God's redemption of Israel from Egypt to her subsequent acceptance of God's laws at Sinai, is key to Judaism's self-understanding and usefully illuminates the meaning of a number of important biblical commandments. Post-biblical Jewish tradition regularly emphasizes that freedom is not found in moving from slavery to personal autonomy, but, counter-intuitively, in being placed under the yoke of God's commandments. The idea that observing God's commandments symbolizes Israel's freedom from slavery is made explicit by the book of Deuteronomy, which directly links a number of commandments including the Sabbath commandment found in Deuteronomy 5 to Israel's being freed from Egyptian bondage.

Finally, as noted in chapter 2 on 'The Torah as a religious book', all Jewish ritual, legal, and ethical practice grows out of and is ultimately grounded in the commandments God gave to Israel at Mount Sinai. Here it is important to highlight that traditional Jews do not see the many commandments of the Torah (613 in total according to Jewish tradition) as onerous, but rather as creating innumerable ways to infuse daily life with holiness and profound meaning.

Examples of Christian use of Exodus

There are many ways in which the Christian tradition has appropriated the book of Exodus and its story. We have mentioned above that Jesus came to be seen as the sacrificial lamb of the Passover, and we should also mention that Matthew 2 connects Jesus to Israel's history when it describes Jesus as God's son taken out of Egypt. But more importantly, it is significant that in the New Testament Jesus is linked to Moses: in a sense, Jesus himself becomes a 'Second Moses'. Not only is Jesus portrayed as a great teacher who affirms many central teachings of the Torah, but he also expounds a new way of life through the giving of a new set of commandments, in some ways more demanding than the Torah itself (given most succinctly in his 'Sermon on the Mount' in Matthew 5–7, perhaps more appropriately titled 'The Torah on the Mount'). Like the teachings of Moses' Torah given to Israel, obedience to the teachings of Jesus is the sign of one's devotion to God, something Jesus makes clear in John's gospel: 'if you love me you will keep my commandments' (14:15).

Jesus, like Moses, meets with God on mountains and here the significance of what Christians call the 'Transfiguration of Jesus' should not be overlooked. In this story, found in the gospels of Matthew, Mark, and Luke, Jesus ascends a mountain and is said to change form (or be 'transfigured'). Here Jesus' face shines like Moses' did after he received the Torah in Exodus 34. What happens next is remarkable. Moses and Elijah, two figures seen to represent the full teachings of Judaism at the time through the Law and the Prophets, appear and are told – by God himself from clouds on the mountain – 'listen to him'. In effect, the gospel writers are attempting to make clear that the teachings of Moses and Elijah (the Torah and the Prophets) are all subservient to Jesus and his teaching. Unfortunately, one negative side effect of this idea is the tendency to neglect or ignore the teachings of Moses rather than to read the Torah in the light of what Jesus taught.

Figure 8 Raphael's *Transfiguration* (1520). Jesus is depicted as elevated above Moses, left, who holds the tablets of the Law, and Elijah, right, who is holding the books of the Prophets

Conclusion

It is often assumed that ancient religious texts are inherently conservative and thus by nature they underwrite the status quo. But Exodus describes the ability of a group of oppressed slaves to successfully challenge a very powerful socio-political system in the name of a higher divine order. Over the course of Western history the Exodus story has often been invoked and has not infrequently brought about revolutionary social changes. Indeed, in the United States in the 1960s this was the story that Martin Luther King Jr placed at the center of the civil rights movement. And elsewhere in the world, a number of theologians created a wider political use of this story in a movement called Liberation Theology, a movement that seeks to reshape society in a more economically just fashion. While one might well ask whether various political uses of the book of Exodus have at times distorted its content to achieve certain social aims, the narrative itself clearly suggests that humans have a God-granted right to challenge tyrants and the political orders that support them.

Having been redeemed from Egypt and received the divine law at Sinai, Israel set about building the portable tent-shrine which in some way creates a movable Mount Sinai, allowing Israel to live in close proximity to God's presence perpetually. But, as we will see, living so close to God requires that Israel maintain a very high level of ritual, ethical, and moral purity. It is these issues that are taken up in the next book, Leviticus, to which we now turn.

6

Leviticus

Introduction and placement in the Torah

Leviticus is the third book of the Pentateuch and thus sits at the very center of the Torah. Its English name is derived from *Liber Leviticus*, a Latinized version of the Septuagint's Greek name for the book, *leuitikon biblion*. Both mean 'book of the Levites'. In time the book came to be known simply as Leviticus, meaning 'pertaining to the Levites'. Jews traditionally call the book *Vayikrah*, 'And he spoke' or possibly 'And he called', after the first Hebrew word of Leviticus, which tells us that God spoke to Moses from the Tent of Meeting. It is more aptly titled in early rabbinic texts as *Torat Kohanim*, 'the Priestly Torah'.

Despite being the shortest book of the Torah (859 verses spread over 27 chapters), for many Christian faith communities it is the least read. Part of this, no doubt, stems from the book's English title, which suggests that Leviticus pertains only to Levites, a group of ancient Israelite religious specialists – people of no particular relevance to the everyday lives of contemporary Christians. However, as we will see, this is misleading. Not only are the Levites mentioned rather sparsely in the book (largely in passing), but more importantly the teachings of the book apply much more broadly and indeed feature prominently in those of Jesus in the New Testament. Leviticus contains principles fundamental not only to Judaism but also to Christians who wish to understand the early Church, most especially the debates that take place between the apostle Paul and his Jewish contemporaries.

Leviticus is primarily a book of instruction, although it contains a few brief narrative interludes. That is, the genre of Leviticus is legal in nature, and law and ritual feature prominently. Contemporary readers tend to have a bias against rules and regulations and thus might be inclined to view Leviticus negatively. Such readers might find the book more accessible if they think of Leviticus as ancient Israel's manual of instruction for daily living. Although there are certainly places where Leviticus appears to be overly concerned with technical legal and ritual details, careful study has often demonstrated that these are part of a larger and richer symbolic understanding of the world. As we discuss below, recent scholarly contributions of anthropologists have shown how various purity and food laws reflect societal attempts to reinforce the cosmos and to encounter the Divine in everyday life.

Overview of Leviticus

Leviticus can be divided into two main blocks, chapters 1–16 (which scholars call the Priestly Code) and chapters 17–26 (referred to as the Holiness Code). There is also an appendix of additional laws found in chapter 27. Chapters 1–7 give detailed information on various sacrificial procedures. Chapters 8–10 describe the inauguration of the sanctuary and the opening sacrificial service. Despite its legal nature, the book does contain occasional narrative asides, such as that found in Leviticus 10:1–11, which relates a story about how a breach in the sacrificial procedures resulted in the death of two of Aaron's sons. Leviticus 11–16 deals with many different types of ritual impurities and touches on a host of topics including: food laws that describe pure and impure animals (chapter 11; we discuss kosher laws below), rules surrounding the ritual impurity that accompanies childbirth (chapter 12), ritual treatment of skin diseases (chapters 13–14), and regulations for normal and abnormal genital discharges (chapter 15). This section concludes with instruction on the yearly Yom Kippur (Day of Atonement) procedures that occupy all of chapter 16. This most sacred day in Israel's calendar is dedicated to ritual cleansing of the sanctuary and removing any sins of the Israelites that were not properly atoned for previously.

The Holiness Code begins in chapter 17 with rules surrounding the consumption of meat. It requires that all domestic animals have their blood dashed upon the sacrificial altar in the sanctuary and that no Israelite or non-Israelite sojourner consume meat with its blood still in it (that is, blood must be properly drained from the slaughtered animal). Leviticus 18 and 20 focus mainly upon illicit sexual unions. Leviticus 19, the heart of the Holiness Code, contains a rich array of ritual and ethical commandments designed to help Israel maintain a holy state. Leviticus 21–2 discusses who may conduct priestly duties and some general rules surrounding these duties. Chapter 23 contains the yearly liturgical calendar and gives a brief description of each sacred occasion. Of note is that the weekly Sabbath is given pride of place as the first holiday in the yearly cycle. Chapter 24 is a hodgepodge of various laws including the rules surrounding the Menorah (or oil lamp) and the showbread (loaves of bread set out once a week in the sanctuary), a short narrative that leads to a new legislative ruling on the question of blasphemy, and it concludes with some general reflections that stress the principle of equality before the law.

Leviticus 25 explains in detail the rules surrounding the sabbatical and Jubilee years, which occur every seventh and fiftieth year respectively. This legislation called for the return of all lands to their original familial owners every fifty years. Chapter 26, in a manner similar to Deuteronomy 27–8, first lists the blessings that will accrue to Israel when she observes the rules found in Leviticus, and then elaborates on the penalties that Israel will suffer for violating her covenantal responsibilities. Finally, chapter 27 is an appendix of laws concerning gifts made to God which also explains how in certain cases one might be able to buy back such sacred gifts by donating their value plus an additional penalty to the sanctuary.

THE YEAR OF JUBILEE

Not only does the Torah specify that Israel is to rest on the seventh day of each week ('Sabbath Day' or 'Shabbat'), but it goes further and stipulates that every seven years the land itself is to rest (called a 'Sabbath Year'). The word *sabbath* appears to be derived from a Hebrew verb meaning 'to cease', and during the Sabbath Year the land was not to be worked. However, a further ordinance is given in Leviticus 25 in which every seventh Sabbath Year was to be a special year of rest called the Year of Jubilee. In this Jubilee Year a particular ram's horn was blown (called a *yovel*; the word Jubilee is a direct borrowing of this Hebrew term) and an additional practice was to be added to the regular Sabbatical Year legislation: all land acquired during the previous nearly half-century was to be returned to its original owner or tribe and all Israelite debts were to be cancelled.

Some scholars doubt if the Jubilee legislation was ever practiced in ancient Israel. However, even if it was only an ideal, it speaks volumes about the Torah's concern to provide correctives that periodically prompt society to reallocate resources that over time tend to end up in the hands of the wealthy few.

Contemporary controversies

The study of Leviticus has been significantly affected by the work of a prominent twentieth-century British anthropologist, Mary Douglas (1921–2007). Her work on purity, danger, ritual, and taboo was ground-breaking. Her theories developed over time (and were modified) but among other things she argued that distinctions in Leviticus regarding purity and pollution are not simply primitive superstitions but rather reveal a complex, ordered system reflecting larger ethical and societal norms. For example, Douglas rejected the widespread idea that the distinctions between clean and unclean animals in Leviticus were arbitrary. These distinctions, according to Douglas, reinforce the created order as reflected in Genesis 1, a text which scholars attribute to the same Priestly authors who produced Leviticus 1–16. In P's view, only animals that fully conform to each of the three realms of creation – sky, land, and sea – are fit for Israelite consumption. As Douglas makes clear, this is because there is a direct correlation between P's conception of holiness and the idea of wholeness. To maintain holiness not only must one avoid unethical behaviors but one must not consume things that are viewed as unwholesome. Thus one avoids eating animals like a pig because pigs do not exhibit all the characteristics of exemplary four-footed domestic land animals, in that unlike cows and sheep they do not chew their cud. As Douglas notes in her book *Purity and Danger*, 'the dietary laws would have been like signs which at every turn inspired meditation on the oneness, purity and completeness of God. By rules of avoidance holiness was given a physical expression in every encounter with the animal kingdom and at every meal' (p. 57).

Another issue related to the study of Leviticus is that of composition. Contemporary critics attribute the two large blocks of Leviticus to distinct sources, both of which belong to the larger Priestly school of writers. Because of the holiness language and ethos of chapters 17–26, scholars now speak of this material as a unified block that they call the 'Holiness Code' (or 'H' for short). The other main section, the Priestly Code (Leviticus 1–16), is generally considered to be penned by the same writer (or writers) of the other P material in the Pentateuch. There are major debates about when each of these sources was written, by whom, and which came first. However, such debates do not significantly affect our discussion on Leviticus, to which we now turn.

The inseparability of ethics and ritual

Almost everyone has heard the injunction, 'You shall love your neighbor as yourself'. However, many people seem unaware that Jesus, who uses this saying in the gospels, is in fact quoting from Leviticus 19:18. Fewer still are aware of the larger context of Leviticus 19 in which this passage sits. Leviticus 19 opens with a miniature version of the Ten Commandments: holding one's parents in awe, keeping the Sabbath, and not worshiping idols (verses 1–4). After some general sacrificial rules (verses 5–8), the passage turns to a number of social issues such as: feeding the poor (verses 9–10), not stealing or lying, not swearing falsely (verse 12), the strong not oppressing the weak and vulnerable (verses 13–14), rendering even-handed justice to all (verse 15), and not slandering one's fellow Israelites (verse 16). Most interesting is that the immediate context of verses 17–18 on loving one's neighbor speaks of the necessity of reproving a neighbor who is acting wrongly even while not taking revenge against him (this perhaps being reserved for the Deity). Clearly the word 'love' in this passage is communicating something more akin to proper treatment of one's fellow citizens than some type of emotion. The emphasis on tactfully reproving a wayward fellow citizen is a far cry from the now widespread idea that loving one's neighbors means not judging them but rather accepting them as they are. It should be noted that the same concern for reproving one's neighbor occurs in the New Testament (Matthew 18:15–20).

This unusual mixture of ritual, moral, and criminal laws – unusual at least to our contemporary sensibilities – continues throughout the rest of Leviticus 19, fleshing out the complexity of the concept of holiness in the Hebrew Bible stressed in the chapter's opening verses. Westerners tend to highlight ethics over ritual and view religion as a matter of personal preference. However, Leviticus conceptualizes holiness as a unity of proper ethical and ritual conduct and it affirms that religion is not a private matter between each individual and God. Much the same can be said about the New Testament. A number of New Testament texts indicate that the early Church also stressed the communal dimensions of religion prevalent here and in the rest of the Bible (for example, see 1 Corinthians 11–14). The priestly authors of Leviticus 19 as well as other major streams of biblical theology envision life as an ongoing encounter between the sacred community and the Divine. As we noted in our discussion of the laws in Exodus 21–3, so here too; an individual who sins against God, whether it be due to a ritual or ethical lapse, also offends and harms his or her community. And when an individual wrongs a fellow citizen, be it in a criminal, civil, or moral matter, it is offensive to God as well as to the larger community. In Leviticus, religion pervades all domains of life rather than being confined to the private sphere as it frequently is in the modern West.

Creating space for the Deity

In Priestly texts, Israel functions as a mediator for God's holiness by creating an environment that permits the Deity to take up residence in the sanctuary. Thus according to Exodus 25 Israel must construct a shrine and its utensils according to a precise model revealed by God to Moses. It also necessitates that various ritual procedures be executed correctly. God's environment was not only affected by the actions or inactions of various cultic officials, but also by any Israelite who even accidentally committed a breach of God's law. In fact, in certain instances even a non-Israelite could pollute God's environment if he or she ate impure things within the land of Israel and refused to follow the levitical rules of purification (see Leviticus 17:15–16). It is on this basis that ancient Israel recognized and accepted a type of communal responsibility.

Oppressive hierarchies or orders of holiness?

Levitical texts are sometimes seen as hegemonic because they presume certain hierarchies between differing groups of Israelites, between various geographical places, as well as between Israel and other nations (see figure 9).

However, viewing the carefully ordered holiness structure of Leviticus as hegemonic is unwarranted and simplistic. Many would suggest that P, and even more so H, did a great deal to ensure that various theological ideas were understood and applied broadly, and without distinction. The fact that Leviticus 19 begins with a call for *all the congregation of the people of Israel* to be holy as God is holy suggests a bold attempt to make Israel a nation of priests. Now every Israelite must maintain not only a higher level

	Very Holy	Holy	Clean	Unclean	Very Unclean
Places	Holy of holies (the innermost section of the sanctuary that housed the ark)	Holy place (the middle section of the sanctuary where one finds the incense altar)	Court (the third section of the sanctuary located outside to accommodate animal sacrifices)	Camp	Outside the camp
People	High priest	Priest	Levites, clean Israelites	People with minor impurities	People with major impurities, the dead
Rituals	Sacrifice (not eaten by people)	Sacrifice (priests eat)	Sacrifice (non-priests eat)	Purification (1 day)	Purification (7 days)
Times	Day of Atonement	Festivals, Sabbath	Common days		

Figure 9 Holiness Continuum in Leviticus

of ritual purity but also higher standards of behavior toward each other because they live in close proximity to the divine presence. In some sense each member of Israel helps mediate the Divine to the larger world. Furthermore, if certain resident aliens wished to participate in living near and helping to mediate the Divine, the Priestly writers make space for such individuals if they are willing to abide by Israel's ritual rules (Exodus 12:48–9 and Leviticus 19:33–4).

HEBREW MATTERS: THE MEANING OF PURITY IN LEVITICUS

Throughout much of Leviticus and in particular in chapters 11–16, the discussion centers on questions of purity and impurity. The terms purity and impurity carry connotations in English that at times interfere with understanding how these terms function in certain biblical passages. In English, when one hears someone or something labeled as impure it often implies that they are of less worth or even that they are sinful or immoral. Thus when we as contemporary readers learn that Leviticus 15 considers a menstruating woman impure, we often bristle and reply that this is a perfectly natural process. Why should something that occurs naturally make one impure?

There is now a growing consensus that within Leviticus 11–16 the terms pure (*tahor*) and impure (*tamai*) are used in a strictly ritual sense to describe passing bodily states. In this view all humans at times experience life-events that make them temporarily impure ritually (not ethically) and ritual procedures are put in place to bring them back to a state of purity. One sees this more clearly when one examines the context surrounding the menstrual laws in Leviticus 15:19–24, a passage discussed below.

The laws in Leviticus concerning clean and unclean range from the general to the more specific. To focus our discussion, we will examine Leviticus 15 in detail. This section presents five pieces of legislation (dealing with various bodily emissions) arranged in an orderly fashion. Leviticus 15:1–15 begins with the case of a man who has an abnormal genital discharge and then verses 16–17 regulate what is to occur if a man has a nocturnal emission, an event the text seems to view as quite natural. Leviticus 15:18 discusses the impurity that arises from sexual intercourse between a man and a woman. Not only is such sexual contact viewed as normal, but it is divinely ordained, for according to P God's first command to humans in Genesis 1 is to be fruitful and multiply. Leviticus 15:19–24 discusses the ritual rules surrounding menstruation, also a completely natural event, although one that women in antiquity experienced with less frequency than women in the modern West due to the numbers of pregnancies, the length of nursing time, and the less protein-rich diets such women experienced in their lives. Leviticus 15:25–30 then turns to irregular female genital flows and the chapter finishes with a summary statement. The fact that one becomes impure through normal intercourse or menstruation demonstrates that, for P, becoming impure is not to be equated with committing a sin or being an inferior person. According to Leviticus 15 becoming impure is not a problem but rather something that occurs periodically throughout one's life. What is considered a sin is failing to observe the rules of impurity and the rituals that move one back to purity.

A matter of life and death

One might still ask, however: if these laws are not aimed at identifying sinners then what are they about? States of impurity symbolize a fracture in the fabric of ordered life. The most likely explanation for many of the laws found in Leviticus 12–15 is that they are attempting to rectify various symbolic encounters with death. In ancient Israel death and life were seen as existing on a continuum and in a certain sense death represented a very diminished form of life. In turn, certain types of sicknesses that diminished one's quality of life were seen as a form of death. This explains why according to Leviticus 13–14 one who experiences a severe skin disease becomes impure and it also explains why a male or a female who has an abnormal genital discharge is impure. Those who suffer from these conditions are living a diminished life.

Now one might ask: well, why does a normal seminal emission, normal menstruation, and normal sexual intercourse make one impure? The answer appears to be that although these are natural bodily functions, they still symbolize an encounter with death. This is most obvious in the case of menstruation which when it occurs indicates a lost chance at a potential pregnancy which could have produced a new life. The logic is likely the same for a nocturnal emission in that it too is a lost chance to procreate.

But what of the case of normal male–female intercourse? Why should this result in one becoming impure? The likely answer is that even while this act may potentially produce a new life, the emission of semen that occurs during this act was likely understood as a waning in the male life force. This belief may have been heightened within biblical culture because the mechanics of semen production and pregnancy were inadequately understood. It may be that underlying this is a belief that a male had a limited amount of seminal fluid and each drop expended would bring him closer to death. Or it may be based more on the widespread recognition that men are often enervated after intercourse. These ideas are still found today in the French euphemism for orgasm, *la petit mort* (or the little death), as well as in the widespread belief that athletes such as boxers are more aggressive if they avoid intercourse before a match.

Examples of Jewish use of Leviticus

It would be difficult to overstate the importance of Leviticus within post-biblical Jewish life. Traditionally, Jewish children begin their study of the Torah with Leviticus. The word Torah means 'teaching' and Leviticus is a book filled with teachings about how one is to live a godly life. Leviticus physically sits in the middle of the Torah and it could be described metaphorically as the heart of the Torah. One of the most obvious places one encounters Leviticus in Jewish life is in the vast array of food or kosher laws found in Jewish practice. On the basis of Leviticus 11, which contains just a basic list of prohibited and permitted animals, in combination with certain other biblical rules such as the prohibition on boiling a young animal in its mother's milk found in Exodus 23 and Deuteronomy 14, the Rabbis developed a complex system of food laws still observed by many Jews today. In a similar fashion, observant Jewish women still adhere to the menstrual purity rules described in Leviticus 15. And as noted in chapter 2, while animal sacrifices are not currently offered, the procedures surrounding the regular sacrificial offerings are included in the liturgy and thus the various sacrifices are symbolically offered.

Perhaps the greatest impact of Leviticus on subsequent Jewish life is the ongoing affirmation within Judaism that spirituality is enriched – not diminished – when it is clothed in ritual practices that tie together the physical and the spiritual worlds. While some might bridle at this thought and argue that such laws seem ridiculous, anthropologists like Mary Douglas have demonstrated how such laws are part of a larger system that seeks to bring humans into regular contact with the Divine by making manifest and reinforcing the created order. The contemporary movement toward eating organic foods and foods that avoid harming the environment is in some sense an affirmation of the fundamental insight of Leviticus that physical holiness begets spiritual holiness.

Examples of Christian use of Leviticus

If it would be difficult to overstate the importance of Leviticus
within Judaism, then it would be difficult to understate its
importance within contemporary Christianity. As mentioned
above, Leviticus seems to receive little attention in mainstream
Christianity, despite being the book to which Jesus points when
asked what is the greatest commandment and one that features
prominently in Paul's teaching as seen in Romans 13 and
Galatians 5. It is not that the book has been overtly discarded or
abrogated, but rather, it is usually simply ignored. Nevertheless,
at times Leviticus is used in debates to support views or practices
that various religious practitioners wish to further. For example,
conservative Christians often point to Leviticus 18:22 to argue
that homosexual practice is a sin, though when pressed these
adherents may have difficulty explaining why other levitical
commandments, such as prohibiting the charging of interest in
Leviticus 25, are apparently no longer binding. Because Christians
believe that portions of the law are fulfilled and no longer apply
to daily life, the Christian interpretation of Leviticus becomes
difficult. Indeed, large portions of the New Testament reveal
attempts to make sense of why certain laws in Leviticus no longer
apply, or do not apply to Gentiles, even while other laws from this
same book remain in force. We discussed some of these problems
in chapter 2 above.

Theologically speaking, however, Christianity has made much
of Leviticus through its understanding of Jesus as the one-time
sacrifice that makes human beings acceptable, or right with God,
a topic discussed in the book of Hebrews in the New Testament.
In Christian thinking, there is no longer a need for a yearly
'Day of Atonement' because that day is thought to have taken
place once-and-for-all in Jesus' sacrificial death, removing the
sins of the human family forever (see Hebrews 9). Further,
it might be argued that the 'Kingdom of God' envisioned in

the New Testament is a time and place where slaves are free, debts are cancelled, land is shared, people listen to God's word, and where peace and rest are experienced everywhere. That is, the Kingdom resembles an extended or everlasting Jubilee. Such links to Leviticus may not be made explicit in the New Testament, but teachings regarding God's Kingdom make much more sense when viewed in light of the principles found in this important book.

Conclusion

Leviticus is much more than an obscure, detailed manual for a small group of ancient Israelite priests. Its implicit and explicit use in both the Jewish and Christian traditions testifies to its dynamic teachings. This short book that sits at the center of the Torah has had immense influence on later Jewish and Christian religious practice. Though its teachings may not be everywhere observed in Judaism and Christianity, its principles have shaped generations of adherents who seek to live rightly before God and to create a community in which God can dwell.

7

Numbers

Introduction and placement in the Torah

Numbers, the fourth book in the Torah, derives its name from the Septuagint or Greek translation of the Torah, there named *Arithmoi*. This term was picked up by Jerome in his Latin Vulgate, where he calls it *Numeri*. The title likely came about due to the fact that Numbers contains two detailed census lists of the twelve tribes of Israel, one in Numbers 1 and another in chapter 26. The title for the book in Jewish tradition, *Bemidbar* or 'In the Wilderness', is derived from the fifth word in Numbers 1:1. This title may capture the content of this book more adequately, inasmuch as the events of the book take place during Israel's forty-year desert sojourn. The 36 chapters of the book contain a total of 1288 verses, making it comparable in length to Exodus.

Numbers continues the story of Israel after the people receive the detailed legal instruction found in Leviticus. By the end of Numbers, the leader Moses is prepared to be replaced by Joshua, and a new generation is ready to enter the Promised Land. The stage is thus set for Deuteronomy, Moses' parting words to Israel before they cross the Jordan River into Canaan.

Overview of Numbers

Numbers can be divided according to several schemes. One set of divisions is based on the locations where the action takes place. In this geographically oriented scheme, Numbers 1:1–10:10

occurs at Mount Sinai, thus linking the first section of the book with the material in Leviticus and the second half of Exodus. The second section, Numbers 10:11–20:13, chronicles Israel's journey from Sinai to Kadesh (an area believed to be north of Sinai, at which Israel spent much of her time in the wilderness). Finally, Numbers 20:14 to the conclusion of the book covers the movement from Kadesh to the plains of Moab (an area immediately north of the Dead Sea, east of the Jordan River), and describes the first stages of Israel's conquest of Canaan, which involves taking certain lands east of the Jordan.

Another way to divide the book is into two halves, based on the placement of the two census lists. In this model, the first census and what follows (chapters 1 to 25) contain the actions of the rebellious generation of Israelites, who all, apart from Caleb and Joshua, end up dying in the wilderness. The second census list in Numbers 26 occurs at the beginning of the materials dealing with the next generation of Israelites who are generally portrayed as obedient and faithful as they initiate the process of conquering the land of Canaan.

A third way to account for the book's structure is by noting that it is composed of blocks of legal and narrative materials in a rotating pattern (or 'ring' structure). Thus 1:1–10:10 is composed primarily of laws, followed by 10:11–14:45, a long narrative block. Next one finds the legally oriented chapter 15 which is followed by another narrative section in 16–17. This pattern continues three more times until the end of the book. Although the subject of some debate, these various schemes suggest that the book was woven together with some care rather than simply containing a loose collection of laws and stories.

Contemporary controversies

However, this last point also conveniently introduces one of the issues often debated within Numbers scholarship: that of coherence and theme. Given that there are three differing and at times competing ways that scholars outline the book may suggest that this material is untidy and difficult to organize. On a surface reading, it could indeed seem that Numbers is not terribly coherent. Unlike the narrative material of Genesis and much of Exodus, and the legal material in Leviticus, Numbers contains a variety of genres and materials all brought together into one whole. We find two detailed census lists, narrative materials regarding Israel's journey, details on priestly duties, a peculiar test for adultery, discussion on who speaks for God and the nature of prophecy, a story of sibling rivalry and unhealthy in-law relations, instructions for Passover, a lengthy, seemingly out-of-place story regarding a foreign seer, laws for life in Canaan, and so on. Paraphrasing Wellhausen, one might be tempted to call it the 'junk-drawer' of the Torah, that is, a book like that one drawer in many people's houses where they put things they otherwise don't know where to store. However, as we shall see, the above three proposed structures do go some distance in helping readers make sense of the book, and these proposals are not mutually exclusive.

The varied nature of Numbers brings up another well-worn debate in Numbers scholarship, that of composition. The diverse material in Numbers could point to multiple sources, perhaps J, E, and P, though the demarcations are not easy to define. For example, the Balaam story in Numbers 22–4 alternates the divine names YHWH and Elohim so frequently that it suggests a single author or editor is using them theologically; this may explain why scholars have had difficulty separating the J and E sources in this passage. Whatever the case, and whatever the historicity of the Numbers material overall, most scholars agree that the book contains much P material.

Problems related to historicity and historical accuracy bring up one final issue for our discussion here, that of large numbers. The issue stems from reports of a rather obviously oversized Israelite populace leaving Egypt and entering the desert. The problem is hinted at in Exodus 12:37 and 38:26, but becomes full-blown in Numbers where we read that, when totaled and women and children are accounted for, some 2,000,000 Israelites leave Egypt. Archeological records indicate that Egypt's army around this time would likely have only had approximately 20,000 men, a force that the 600,000 Israelite soldiers that Numbers 1:46 counts could have easily overpowered. To put matters in perspective, even conservative scholars admit that 2,000,000 people leaving Egypt would entail, based on the land's geography, a line of people that would extend over 100 miles long. Depending on where the Reed Sea is located, this would mean that the last of the Israelites would only begin to cross it as the first Israelites arrive at Kadesh. Such large numbers make Israel's departure from Egypt seem less of a miracle and are at odds with the Hebrew Bible's emphasis on Israel being a small people, a people needing to increase in number before it could take the Promised Land (Exodus 23:30).

Solutions do not come easily. Perhaps the numbers are hyperbolic or superlative in order to stress Israel's divine blessing, something texts such as Exodus 1:7 and Numbers 22:3 suggest. Alternatively, according to some scholars the Hebrew word *eleph*, used to indicate 1000, could instead represent military or family units, thus bringing the number down to approximately 6000 soldiers or 20,000 Israelites in total. Such numbers would be more in line with population estimates for the ancient Near East at the time.

At Mount Sinai: Numbers 1–10

As noted in the overview, Numbers begins with a lengthy block of legal materials that runs from 1:1 to 10:10. Chapters 1–2 include the first census list, followed by the plan for how the various tribes will encamp as they get ready to leave Sinai and move through the wilderness toward the Promised Land. Chapters 3–4 contain the rules surrounding how the priests and Levites were to transport the various parts of the portable tent-shrine. Numbers 5 has several pieces of legislation, the longest of which is a special ritual procedure that a husband can impose on his wife if he suspects her of being unfaithful to him (see text box below). Numbers 6 contains the rules surrounding the nazirite, a person who takes a special vow to refrain from ingesting alcoholic or grape products, not to cut one's hair, and to avoid corpse impurities for a set length of time. Based on Judges 13 and Luke 1:15 it seems clear that Samson and John the Baptist were nazirites. Chapter 7 rehearses the dedication ceremony that Israel celebrated when she first set up the Tent of Meeting, while chapter 8 explains the unusual status and function of the Levites. Numbers 9 mainly discusses rules for celebrating Passover at a later time, when one might have been prevented from celebrating it at its normal time. Numbers 10 describes Israel's first movements away from Sinai.

THE UNFAITHFUL WIFE OR JEALOUS HUSBAND?

Probably no passage in the Torah repels modern sensitivities more than the *Sotah* (unfaithful wife) text of Numbers 5:11–31. Of the 613 commandments that rabbinic Judaism finds in the Torah, perhaps none seems more primitive and magical in its orientation. If a man suspects that his wife has been unfaithful, he can take her to the priest who will perform a ritual that includes the preparation of a potion made from water, sweepings from the tabernacle floor, and some curses written in ink dissolved into the water that the woman must drink. If she becomes unwell (through stomach bloating or other bodily deterioration), she is guilty. If she experiences no illness, she is innocent.

THE UNFAITHFUL WIFE OR JEALOUS HUSBAND? (cont.)

It is difficult to know what to make of this legislation and it is obvious that ancient gender imbalances permeate it (for example, there is no similar law for the woman who suspects her husband of adultery). More recently commentators have noticed that the law of the *Sotah*, though it may seem out of place, may well be part of a larger theme in Numbers: the deterioration of trust. Israel is regularly portrayed as a people who will not fully trust God and within Israel there is a good deal of interpersonal distrust. Thus in Numbers 11 certain people are jealous to guard Moses' prophetic abilities from others who appear to speak by God's spirit, and in Numbers 12, even Miriam and Aaron come to distrust their brother Moses as leader, becoming jealous of his position. Similar jealousies recur in Numbers 16–17. In all these instances *the untrusting, jealous parties are wrong*. Perhaps the *Sotah* legislation is in fact a subtle criticism of the husband who does not trust his wife. In other words, the point of the *Sotah* may relate to the breakdown of trust between two parties that should be most trusting (spouses) or, applied metaphorically to the larger book of Numbers, God and Israel.

Complaints, strife, and death: Numbers 11–25

In Numbers 11 one finds what appears to be two major narratives that have been woven together. One thread is a second retelling of the manna and quails stories, which were first reported in Exodus 16 when Israel had just come out of Egypt. However, in Exodus 16 the manna story is lengthy and the quails are mentioned in passing; further, generally speaking the tale has a happy ending. Here in Numbers, however, the quail story is told in much greater detail and it now concludes with a punishment.

These paired stories are part of a larger cycle of complaint that animates some of Exodus and much of Numbers. Within this story in Numbers, a separate narrative strand relates how the overburdened Moses was able to distribute his charismatic authority to a wider group of seventy tribal elders.

The theme of Moses' authority is taken up once again in Numbers 12, which recounts how Miriam and Aaron spoke against Moses, and were reprimanded, with Miriam receiving a severe, near deadly punishment. This chapter contains one of the clearest statements in the Torah of Moses' unique prophetic status in that Moses hears through direct divine–human speech; however, the text also specifies that God extends lesser gifts of prophecy to others via dreams and visions. The theme of 'who speaks for God' in this passage may well be a larger one for Numbers in that we see it revisited again in Numbers 16–17 as well as in the Book of Balaam found in Numbers 22–4.

Numbers 13–14 is certainly one of the most memorable narratives in the book. This passage recounts how God commanded the Israelites to send spies (or scouts) into Canaan and how these spies, apart from Caleb and Joshua, brought back a negative report that led the Israelites to reject God's command to take possession of what would become the land of Israel. In turn, God once more considered destroying the Israelites and starting over by building a new nation from Moses and his future descendants. Moses, in a heroic act of intercession similar to Exodus 32–4, is able to convince God to relent and refrain from wiping Israel out completely. However, in this case the rebellious generation is condemned to die in the wilderness and would therefore not see the land they refused to go up and conquer. This is the explanation given in Numbers for the Israelites' extended stay in the desert, lasting for forty years.

After Numbers 15, a chapter of loosely related laws primarily concerning sacrificial procedures, chapters 16–17 contain yet another pair of intertwined stories of distrust and rebellion. One storyline involves Dathan and Abiram who challenge Moses' authority once more and the other strand tells the story of Korah and 250 Levites who question the special status of Aaron. The theme of a distrustful and rebellious people steadily grows in these chapters. One can also see that a host of narratives in Numbers wrestle with the ways in which religion and politics intersect.

Numbers 18 details the rules surrounding the special privileges that the Torah accords to priests and Levites to help support them and chapter 19 discusses the rules of the Red Heifer, an animal whose ashes were used in various purification procedures. Numbers 20 and 21 narrate several loosely related stories mainly about the transition between generations and the beginnings of the conquest of the land of Canaan. Chapter 20 begins with Miriam's death and then tells another story of rebellion, in which an explanation is given as to why God did not permit Moses to enter the Promised Land. Moses himself, like his generation, seems to rebel and usurp God's power in an episode in which he strikes a rock with his staff to find water, though the specifics of his offense are unclear (as many as ten different explanations have been proposed by medieval Jewish commentators). After narrating the negative response of the Edomites to Israel's request to pass through their territory, this passage ends with Aaron's death. Numbers 21 begins and ends with reports of successful battles while traveling through lands east of the Jordan River and the material in between narrates the unusual story of the poisonous snakes God sends and the miraculous cure God reveals to Moses.

HEBREW MATTERS: SNAKES ON A POLE

Numbers 21:4–9 recounts a tale in which the Israelites murmur against God and Moses by complaining about the harsh wilderness conditions, specifically the lack of water and variety of foods.

HEBREW MATTERS: SNAKES ON A POLE (*cont.*)

God sends a plague against the Israelites in the form of fiery snakes, or in Hebrew *seraphim*. This same Hebrew word is found in Isaiah 6 to describe snake-like angelic beings that are part of God's heavenly retinue. The threat of the fiery snakes in Numbers is overcome when Moses crafts a bronze snake and places it on a pole, which Israelites look to when bitten to be healed. We know from 2 Kings 18 that the same bronze snake was placed in the temple until the time of Hezekiah. In light of the fact that Isaiah's vision in the temple takes place before Hezekiah destroys this statue, it seems likely that this snake 'comes to life' in Isaiah's vision.

Numbers 22–4 recounts the story of Balak, the King of Moab, who hires a professional diviner named Balaam to put a hex on the people of Israel. This highly entertaining story, which includes a talking donkey, relates how Balak's attempt to curse Israel is unsuccessful. And, as mentioned, it picks up the theme of prophecy and divine speech through its continual references to only speaking what YHWH permits. In the end, Balaam delivers some of the most profound blessings and prophecies concerning the Israelites found anywhere in scripture. It is remarkable not only that such words come from a non-Israelite, but that this non-Israelite later becomes one of the most reviled characters in later Jewish and Christian texts (see for example 2 Peter 2:15–16; Jude 11; Revelation 2:14).

Numbers 25 tells the last story of the Sinai generation, directly before the census list in chapter 26 that introduces a new, non-rebellious people. This chapter tells of a strange incident in which certain Israelites intermingle with Midianite women (and worship their gods), in turn resulting in a plague that breaks out as a punishment. The climax of the story takes place when the priest Phinehas takes radical action and kills an Israelite man and a

Midianite woman – apparently in the middle of their defiant and flamboyant sexual act – thus stopping the plague. The rebels are killed and Phinehas is in turn granted a special covenantal relationship with God.

A new generation: Numbers 26–36

Chapter 26 contains the second census list in this book, which, after cataloguing its precise numbers, makes clear that apart from Caleb and Joshua (the faithful spies): 'among these there was not one of those enrolled by Moses and Aaron the priest, who had enrolled the Israelites in the wilderness of Sinai' (Numbers 26:64). The reason? That generation 'shall die in the wilderness' as decreed by God (Numbers 26:65). From a logistical point of view such an idea is untenable, in that generations do not start and stop every forty years, and it is remarkable that unlike the former generation – which was marked by punishment and death – there is not one Israelite death reported in the rest of Numbers. It is also remarkable that an obvious transition takes place in that contrary to the former generation that murmured and rebelled continually, this new generation is one that does not complain but rather negotiates with Moses and God to find solutions that suit all parties involved.

Following the census, Numbers 27 begins by discussing a legal innovation that permits women to inherit land in certain instances. This legal modification is in turn contested in Numbers 36, where a new twist is added that still permits women to inherit property but prohibits them from marrying outside their particular tribal group (thus the land always remains within the original tribe). Chapter 27 ends by narrating the passing of Moses' authority to Joshua. Both of these episodes show that the Torah is a platform for the ongoing life of the people of Israel, and that the Torah is part of a living and changing tradition. It is worth noting that many of the arguments between various groups of later Jews and Christians are not over whether the tradition can be adapted to new circumstances, but over how and when such innovations should occur.

WOMEN'S VOICES IN THE TORAH

As discussed in chapter 3, there have been many recent attempts to present fuller and more complex treatments of women in the Bible through re-examining texts that have been underemphasized or unnoticed in the past. In the story of the daughters of Zelophehad found in Numbers 27, it is noteworthy that although ancient convention would have resisted women speaking out publicly against their leaders, the daughters of Zelophehad here do exactly that and demand that property be given to them. Moses presents their case to God and God takes their side. While it is sometimes asserted that the Torah is a document produced by men for men, the actions of these women testify to the fact that women's voices are not only present in the Torah, but at times were instrumental in shaping the biblical legal tradition.

The remaining material in Numbers moves between narrative sequences and legal material. Numbers 28–9 outlines the sacrifices that the priests in Israel are to offer daily, on Sabbaths, and on various holidays. Numbers 30 takes up various issues surrounding oaths, especially those made by women, in which money or valuables are dedicated to God. Despite a provision whereby a father or husband could annul a woman's vow if done so immediately, such vows otherwise stand perpetually. Furthermore, no man is permitted to annul the vows of a widowed or divorced woman. Although still revealing gender imbalances, it is noteworthy that these texts accord women important protections in this patriarchal environment.

This last section of Numbers describes Israel's slaughter of Midian, the very people who led Israel astray in Numbers 25. Thus this episode may symbolize the new generation's victory over religious temptation. Following this is instruction for apportioning the land to the Israelite tribes. The tribes of Reuben and Gad ask to remain in the land east of the Jordan (an area not originally envisioned as part of the Promised Land) and Moses becomes irate. Unlike the old generation that murmured and rebelled, this new generation responds calmly and negotiates. They make a convincing case to Moses, agreeing to support the rest of Israel in conquering the remaining land of Canaan before settling in their homes east of the Jordan. The stage is now set for Moses' parting words to this new generation, a speech that occupies all of Deuteronomy which follows.

Examples of Jewish use of Numbers

There are many places in Jewish life where one encounters materials drawn from Numbers. Perhaps this is most especially true of the imprint Numbers has left on Jewish liturgical practice. Here one thinks of the priestly blessing found in Numbers 6:22–7:

> The LORD spoke to Moses, saying: Speak to Aaron and his sons, saying, Thus you shall bless the Israelites: You shall say to them, The LORD bless you and keep you; the LORD make his face to shine upon you, and be gracious to you; the LORD lift up his countenance upon you, and give you peace. So they shall put my name on the Israelites, and I will bless them.

The significance of this prayer through the ages becomes readily apparent from the fact that, as mentioned in chapter 1, our oldest

Figure 10 The traditional hand-gesture made by Jewish priests upon blessing the people, as seen on the doors of the Alte Synagogue in Essen, Germany. Courtesy Aaron Olaf Batty

known fragment of a biblical text is of this passage and it is found on a tiny (and likely costly) silver scroll that was worn as an amulet. In traditional Orthodox settings, this prayer is still chanted by those of priestly lineage on certain occasions. In fact, when priests say this blessing formally, they split their fingers apart to form the Hebrew letter *shin*, the first letter of one of God's names, *Shaddai*, often translated as *God Almighty*. This particular hand motion (see figure 10) is now widely recognized because Mr Spock on *Star Trek* used it in slightly modified form as the Vulcan greeting gesture. The priestly blessing, minus any hand gestures, is also invoked by parents when blessing their children every Friday night at the Sabbath meal.

Another passage from Numbers with an important place in the liturgy is Numbers 10:35: 'Whenever the ark set out, Moses would say, "Arise, O LORD, let your enemies be scattered, and your foes flee before you."' This passage is part of the regular Torah liturgy and is recited when the Torah scroll is removed from the synagogue ark.

Finally, Numbers 15:37–41 has also left a deep imprint on Jewish life and liturgy. This text, recited as the third paragraph in the *Shema* (the central Jewish prayer that begins 'Hear, O Israel' discussed in detail in chapter 8), contains the commandment to make fringes on one's garment. Jews today continue to wear a tasseled prayer shawl or *tallit* during morning prayer services, and observant Jewish men wear an undergarment called a *tallit katan*, or *tzitzit*, that has fringes on its four corners (see Figure 11).

Examples of Christian use of Numbers

It might be thought that Numbers occupies little space in the Christian tradition. On a surface reading, there are only a few direct references to the book in the New Testament – for instance mention of Balaam, said to be greedy and have had evil intent. When read more closely, however, one will find that the New Testament assumes the story of Numbers and alludes to it often. Prime examples can be found in 1 Corinthians 10 and Hebrews 3–4. Within these texts we find numerous subtle references to Numbers and its story of the generation that was denied entry into Canaan because of rebellion. The message to the Church is always clear: stand firm, have faith, and be diligent to enter God's rest.

One interesting use of Numbers in the New Testament stands out, that of Jesus and Moses' bronze snake. John 3:16, perhaps the most famous passage of the New Testament, is prefaced by

Figure 11 Example of a *tallit*, worn here in prayer at the Western Wall in Jerusalem. The partially visible object on the man's forehead is a phylactery (or *tefillin*), a small box containing verses from the Torah worn by Jewish men during weekday morning services. Courtesy Dan Blumenthal

words that use an analogy to depict Jesus as the snake that was lifted up:

> And just as Moses lifted up the serpent in the wilderness, so must the Son of Man be lifted up, that whoever believes in him may have eternal life. For God so loved the world that he gave his only Son, so that everyone who believes in him may not perish but may have eternal life.
>
> (John 3:14–16)

It is worth noting that although serpents generally are viewed negatively in the Jewish and Christian traditions, it is not the case here. Of course, here Jesus is seen not so much as a snake but as the *seraph* (from *seraphim*, discussed above), which was raised and healed the Israelites when they looked up to it. Early Church Fathers interpret the Numbers passage in light of John's gospel reading. Justin Martyr (100–165 CE), for example, asks why God would instruct Moses to violate the Torah's commandment not to make a graven image of anything in the heavens above or on the earth below. Justin suggests that Moses was to do so because he is announcing the great mystery of the one (Jesus) who would come to break the power of the serpent, and thus the sin that came through Adam. Of course his reading is distinctly Christian and open to debate. However, Justin's words reveal the ingenious ways Christians interpret the Old Testament in the light of the New Testament, not unlike certain Jewish attempts to reinterpret the Torah creatively in the light of later rabbinical teachings.

Finally, Numbers and its stories of Israel in the wilderness have regularly featured in Christian worship. Hymns such as 'Guide Me O Thou Great Redeemer' liken the Christian community to ancient Israel in that both are led by God himself to a promised land. Further, as in the Jewish tradition, the priestly blessing found in Numbers 6:22–7 (also called the Blessing of Aaron) is frequently invoked in Christian worship. The blessing is found in many liturgies, and ministers of Protestant (particularly Reformed) churches will often use the blessing to conclude a worship service or as a dismissal. It is interesting that both Jews and Christians stand united in having this blessing spoken over them so often, though in differing contexts.

Conclusion

The book of Numbers can strike the first-time reader as a mishmash of stories, laws, prophecies, instructions, and other tidbits of information. However, there are several recurring themes that unify the book. In particular, the themes of the deterioration of trust and rebellion permeate the first 25 chapters, while trust and negotiation mark the final section of chapters 26–36. Each section begins with a census and both generations, wicked and good, are the ancestors of Israel, and thus the foreparents of contemporary Jews and Christians. Both groups have recognized that within each generation of its people comes tendencies to rebel and not trust, yet also to listen and obey. There is a tension here, and both communities can see their own fluctuating place within the story. The message of Numbers is to avoid the pitfalls of the past and walk in the ways of those who learn to trust and obey.

8

Deuteronomy

Introduction and placement in the Torah

Deuteronomy is the fifth and final book of the Torah. Its English name comes from the Vulgate, the Latin translation made by Jerome, and literally means the 'second law' (*deuteros nomos*). While this is somewhat accurate in that Deuteronomy contains a second telling of many laws given earlier in the Torah, the exact phrase is drawn from Jerome's rather wooden rendering of an expression found in Deuteronomy 17:18, *mishneh torah*, which might be better translated 'copy of the law'. Jews traditionally call the book *Devarim*, 'words', after the second Hebrew word of Deuteronomy 1:1. Deuteronomy contains 955 verses spread over 34 chapters.

Overview of Deuteronomy

Deuteronomy can be divided into four main sections: (1) an extended recital of the events that Israel experienced during Moses' lifetime that runs from chapter 1 to 11; (2) a large block of legal materials that occupies chapters 12–26; (3) a set of blessings and curses found in chapters 27–8, which are pronounced upon those who will observe or disobey the commandments; and (4) some final instructions and poems from Moses that foretell the future and report Moses' death (chapters 29–34). However, some scholars prefer to divide the book differently, resulting in a five- or six-part structure. From a narrative perspective, Deuteronomy might best be viewed as Moses' last will and testament to his people Israel. In a way unlike the rest of the Torah, Deuteronomy reads as if it is one long speech, or sermon, from the mouth of Moses prior to his death and Israel's entering Canaan. Some have called it Moses' farewell speech.

Contemporary controversies

Almost all modern critics believe that Deuteronomy contains a unique vocabulary that can be traced to a school of thinkers responsible for the religious reform of Judah in the late seventh century BCE. It is believed that the book supposedly discovered in the Jerusalem temple during Josiah's reign (640–609 BCE) contained some form of Deuteronomy (see 2 Kings 22–3 for the fuller story). So, although the book is framed as the last will and testament of Moses, much of its content actually addresses Israelite life in seventh-century BCE Judah.

Most scholars also accept some form of Martin Noth's ground-breaking thesis that the authors of Deuteronomy were also responsible for the theological themes and coherence of the six historical books that follow it. Because of this perceived continuity in themes and emphasis, scholars now call the block of historical books following Deuteronomy (Joshua, Judges, 1 and 2 Samuel, and 1 and 2 Kings) the 'Deuteronomistic History'. It is argued that the theme that runs throughout this material and ties it together is the doctrine of retribution; that is, one will reap what one sows: if the people obey the covenant, they will be blessed; if they do not, they will be cursed. Israel is presented with a life and death choice, as is made clear throughout Deuteronomy (see especially Deuteronomy 28 as well as 30:15–20). The larger Deuteronomistic History, which narrates the history of Israel from Joshua's time through the fall of the Kingdom of Judah in the sixth century BCE, might be viewed as a collection of writings that seek to address 'what went wrong', or why Israel is in a difficult situation. More specifically, why did Israel and Judah go into exile?

An additional issue regularly raised in relation to Deuteronomy and the Deuteronomistic History is how many times these books were edited and to what extent one can correlate these editorial stages with periods in Israel's history. Whatever the editorial process, some would suggest that Deuteronomy coheres with the following historical books so well that we should not speak of a 'Pentateuch' (that is, *five* books of the Torah) but rather a 'Tetrateuch', a section of *four* books, Genesis through Numbers. Deuteronomy thus comes to belong to the books that follow (Joshua through 2 Kings). Although these proposals can be helpful for understanding the development of the Hebrew Bible, one can read the first eleven books of the Bible as a continuous narrative from Eden to Babylon.

Two other important scholarly debates deserve mention. Firstly, the study of Deuteronomy has been illuminated by the discovery and translation of a number of ancient Near Eastern treaties in which various emperors lay out the terms of their relationship to various smaller powers. Scholars refer to these as suzerainty-vassal treaties. There is general agreement that the overarching structure of Deuteronomy resembles patterns found in these Near Eastern treaties. It seems that when Israel looked for language to express her relationship to God, her sovereign, she borrowed models from the wider Near Eastern diplomatic realm. Secondly, scholars continue to argue over whether the laws in Deuteronomy pre- or post-date various laws found in Leviticus.

DEUTERONOMY AND ANCIENT NEAR EASTERN TREATIES

In the middle of the twentieth century, a number of scholars began to argue that Deuteronomy shares much in common with treaty

DEUTERONOMY AND ANCIENT NEAR EASTERN TREATIES (cont.)

documents of the ancient Near East, particularly Hittite (an empire located in Asia Minor, or today's Turkey) suzerainty-vassal treaties of the fourteenth century BCE. These treaties follow a relatively fixed format and read like ancient legal documents. They typically (1) introduce the parties involved, (2) give the historical background of their relationship, (3) list the conditions of the treaty, (4) explain the terms for the public reading and storing of the document, (5) include a call for witnesses (often divinities), and (6) conclude with blessings and curses, based on each party's compliance or failure to comply with the conditions.

Some assert that Deuteronomy followed the Hittite conventions so closely that the book should be viewed as contemporary to the Hittite documents. This would place the authorship of Deuteronomy firmly in the mid-second millennium BCE, or generally in the time when Moses would have walked the earth. We also noted earlier that Deuteronomy can be divided in a manner that correlates the book's format to that found in these ancient treaties:

Hittite suzerainty-vassal treaties	Deuteronomy
1. Introduction/preamble	»» Deuteronomy 1:1–5
2. Historical background	»» Deuteronomy 1:6–3:29
3. Conditions/stipulations	»» Deuteronomy 4–26
4. Publication/public reading	»» Deuteronomy 27:1–10; 31:9–13
5. Divine/other witnesses	»» Deuteronomy 30:15–20; 31:19–22
6. Blessing and curse formula	»» Deuteronomy 28

However, the analogies drawn between Deuteronomy and these Hittite treaties are sometimes forced or inexact, and it is of no real surprise that the strongest arguments along these lines came from those with religious motivation to 'prove' that Moses authored the Pentateuch. Many today find the parallels to be less convincing

> **DEUTERONOMY AND ANCIENT NEAR EASTERN TREATIES (*cont.*)**
>
> than originally proposed and some have argued that the language, phrasing, and treaty format of Deuteronomy resembles more the seventh-century BCE Assyrian state treaties of Esarhaddon than those of the fourteenth-century Hittites. Still, there is broad agreement that in Deuteronomy Israel expressed her formal relationship to God in terms drawn from the wider Near Eastern political realm. While today many politicians invoke religious language in their speeches, here we see the appropriation of ideas drawn from the political realm to express a religious concept.

Retelling Israel's history: Deuteronomy 1–11

Deuteronomy 1–11 contains a recitation of Israel's history, and it retells this history in a new and unique way using a number of highly innovative literary forms. It begins with a scene in which God tells Moses it is time for the Israelites to leave the Mount Sinai area (in Deuteronomy's distinct vocabulary the mountain is often called Horeb) and begin their journey to take possession of the land of Canaan. Through the course of chapters 1–3, Moses narrates the events that occurred between the revelation of the law at Sinai and the current moment in which Moses is about to turn his command over to Joshua. This includes a brief recital of the story of the spies that resulted in Israel's extended stay in the wilderness. According to Deuteronomy 1:34–7, Israel's initial failure to obey God and conquer Canaan made God angry at Moses, causing God to prohibit him from leading the Israelites into Canaan (as noted earlier, Numbers 20 presents a different rationale for God not allowing Moses to enter Canaan). The text proceeds to explain how Israel conquered certain lands that lay east of the Jordan, along the way noting that God strictly prohibited Israel from taking any Edomite or Moabite territory. In Deuteronomy, these peoples – kinsmen of Abraham as well – are protected by God and thus not to be attacked in an offensive war.

Chapters 4–7 then turn back in time to retell the events surrounding the revelation at Mount Sinai. Chapter 4 involves a long speech highlighting the central command to be loyal to God and to avoid any form of idolatry. Chapter 5 contains a repetition of the Ten Commandments with a few slight variations from the version in Exodus 20. Deuteronomy 6 returns to the theme of loyalty to Israel's God and avoidance of becoming ensnared by various idolatrous practices the Israelites might encounter when they enter Canaan.

Deuteronomy 6:4, the closest thing to a Jewish creedal formula, is called the *Shema*: 'Hear [Hebrew *shema*], O Israel: The LORD is our God, The LORD alone.' As noted in our section on 'The liturgical use of the Torah in Judaism' (chapter 2), this formula is a part of the regular prayer liturgy and is also used in certain ritual objects such as the *mezuzah* mounted on doorposts in Jewish homes and buildings. These words have been spoken by Jewish martyrs through the centuries, inasmuch as one of the commandments that one should die for, rather than violate, is the prohibition to commit idolatry.

Chapter 7 continues reflecting on the dangers and lure of idolatry, and thus invokes strong language commanding the Israelites to eradicate the Canaanites and their idolatrous culture. Some have recently argued that the command to annihilate the Canaanites and their culture was likely a metaphor stressing the importance of worshiping God with an undivided heart. As noted earlier, this text was likely composed in the seventh-century BCE, at a time when few ethnically distinct Canaanites would have existed. Still, the use of the violent metaphor of total annihilation of another people, and the fact that this metaphorical text has been invoked over the course of history to brand various groups as worthy of annihilation, suggests that certain biblical texts remain deeply problematic.

HEBREW MATTERS: WHAT DOES THE MOST IMPORTANT PASSAGE MEAN?

No other passage in the Bible, whether Jewish Tanakh or two-Testament Christian Bible, can rightly claim to have the significance and influence that Deuteronomy 6:4–9 does. Not only have these words been repeated each morning and evening by observant Jews for millennia, but when Jesus was asked what the most important commandment is, he immediately quoted from this passage (see Mark 12:28–31; Matthew 22:34–40). Our concern here, however, involves the Hebrew of the *Shema*, and it is remarkable that a centerpiece of Jewish and Christian theology is not straightforward, but ambiguous, in meaning.

Leaving aside debates as to where the *Shema* ends, there is little question that its central teaching is contained in the first statement: 'Hear, O Israel, The LORD is our God, the LORD alone.' The problem is that although the first two words are clear (*shema yisrael*; Hear, O Israel), the following four words are not: *YHWH eloheinu, YHWH echad* (pronounced in Jewish prayer as *adonai eloheinu, adonai echad*). Quite literally, the words translate: 'YHWH our-God, YHWH one [or alone]'. The ambiguity arises here because in Hebrew, as in other ancient languages, the relationship between subject and predicate is often implied rather than stated. It is unclear, therefore, where the reader or translator should insert the word 'is'. There are four main options, as listed in the footnotes of many Bibles:

1. The LORD our God, the LORD is one. (NIV)
2. The LORD is our God, the LORD alone. (NRSV, NJPS)
3. The LORD our God is one LORD. (KJV)
4. The LORD is our God, the LORD is one. (NASB)

**HEBREW MATTERS: WHAT DOES THE MOST
IMPORTANT PASSAGE MEAN? (*cont.*)**

We will not resolve this translational difficulty here; rather, our aim is to highlight just how different each of these grammatically acceptable translations is. In option one, the nature of God is stressed, in that it teaches us that Israel's God, YHWH, is 'one' (or perhaps 'unique' or of 'one essence'). The second option stresses a relationship, one that is exclusive: YHWH is Israel's God and no one else. The third option may seem strained, though in antiquity it was common for a deity to be associated with various locales, thus making it possible for there to be many YHWHs. This translation clears away any debate; there is only one YHWH, not many. The fourth translation provides a combination of options one and two, stressing both the nature of God (YHWH is one) and the idea that *he* (not another) is Israel's God.

This important passage has had a tremendous influence on Judaism and Christianity, and it has contributed to each tradition's understanding of God and the issue of whether monolatry or monotheism best describes Israel's religious outlook. Perhaps part of the attraction and intrigue of this passage is its potential multiple meanings. It is not out of character for Judaism and Christianity to have a central teaching with a meaning that can be debated.

Deuteronomy 8 contains one of the most interesting and profound sermons in Deuteronomy. While Deuteronomy 1 seems aware of the tradition from Numbers in which the forty-year wilderness sojourn is portrayed as a punishment for Israel's disobedience, Deuteronomy 8 offers a very different view of the time Israel spent in the desert. Here, God led Israel for forty years to test them to see if they would obey God. Furthermore, in the harsh desert environment Israel could easily recognize God's power because he fed them with the manna. In this speech Moses invokes a famous expression: 'man does not live by bread alone'.

It is important, however, to note the larger context of this phrase:

> [God] humbled you by letting you hunger, then by feeding you with manna, with which neither you nor your ancestors were acquainted, in order to make you understand that one does not live by bread alone, but by every word that comes from the mouth of the LORD.
>
> (Deuteronomy 8:3)

Chapter 8 then continues by emphasizing that even while God wants to bring Israel into the land so that they can experience its fertility and blessing, doing so involves the danger that Israel might forget God once the people are no longer dependent on God's daily ration of manna. Here the very reward that God wishes to grant to Israel might lead to her undoing.

Chapters 9–10 then rehearse Israel's sin during the Golden Calf episode, further reinforcing the importance of fidelity to God. Chapter 11 in many ways is a summation of chapters 1–10.

Retelling Israel's Law: Deuteronomy 12–26

There is a vast array of legislation in this block of material, some of it reinforcing or slightly modifying legal materials found elsewhere in the Torah, some of it strongly challenging or even overturning certain legal precedents, and some of it found only here and nowhere else. There are a number of important legislative innovations which we will touch upon in our discussion, including the centralization of worship at one shrine, making Israelite worship and society more egalitarian, and the introduction of humane rationalizations for certain laws.

WHY RETELL THE TORAH?

An obvious question comes to mind, especially when we read texts like the Ten Commandments in Deuteronomy 5 – virtually a verbatim retelling of Exodus 20 – and the laws of Deuteronomy 12–26, many of which overlap with laws found in Exodus 21–3 and in Leviticus. Why retell these laws? Why a 'deuteros-nomos' (second-law)? Such questions are not easy to answer, and the matter becomes more complicated when one realizes that Deuteronomy at times modifies, overturns, or simply omits legislation occurring elsewhere in the Torah.

One important theory is that the Torah must be renegotiated with each new generation. As argued in our chapter on Numbers, there is an emphasis on a new generation of Israelites, those who will enter the land, and they need to commit to the covenant as their parents did at Sinai back in Exodus 19–24. Deuteronomy 5:3 drives this point home in an interesting way when it refuses to allow time to advance; it states that God gave the Torah to this very people, even though it is clear that the people hearing these words is a new generation that was not present at Horeb. Passages like Deuteronomy 29 emphasize that each new generation is to commit to the Torah through renewing the covenant. Each generation of Israelites itself stands at Sinai and is to engage the Torah anew. In learning to negotiate its teachings, each new generation must commit to it actively. The long stream of rabbinic teaching on the Torah testifies to this principle as well.

In terms of unique materials, one of the most unusual types of laws found in Deuteronomy 12–26 is what might be termed early environmental legislation. Deuteronomy 20:19–20 prohibits the unnecessary destruction of the natural environment during warfare and 22:6–7, which prohibits the taking of a mother bird along with her young or eggs, attempts to prevent the total decimation of an animal population.

An example of reinforcing a pre-existing law with slight modifications can be found in the prohibitions surrounding the planting of mixed grains in one field, plowing with two different animals, and wearing of mixed garments. These are all mentioned in Leviticus 19:19 in very terse form. Deuteronomy 22:9–11 appears to fill out these rules by applying them not only to grain fields but to vineyards as well, by further noting that plowing with two differing animals applies specifically to yoking an ox and donkey together, and by specifying that wearing mixed garments is limited to a wool and linen combination. It is difficult to know if Deuteronomy is changing the legislation found in Leviticus or is simply repeating the laws found in this part of Leviticus in fuller form but in full agreement with the original intent of Leviticus.

There are indeed examples in which Deuteronomy rather radically changes certain laws found elsewhere in the Torah. Thus Deuteronomy 14:21 permits an Israelite to sell meat to a resident alien from an animal that died of natural causes rather than from being purposefully slaughtered. This law stands in direct contradiction to Leviticus 17:15 which requires resident aliens (just like Israelites) to avoid ingesting meat from animals that died on their own, or if they do eat such meat to engage in a purification ritual normally reserved for Israelites alone.

IS DEUTERONOMY MORE EGALITARIAN?

In looking at Deuteronomy's various retellings of laws also found in Exodus, some have noticed a pattern toward, among other things, more egalitarian modes of life and worship. Two examples stand out. The first involves the release of Hebrew slaves. In antiquity, a person who owed a debt to another, but could not repay it, might sell him or herself (or a son or daughter) into 'debt slavery'. This was often regulated so that it was not abused, but it is interesting that the once preferential treatment

IS DEUTERONOMY MORE EGALITARIAN? (cont.)

of male slaves is adjusted in Deuteronomy to include women. Deuteronomy 15:12–17, for instance, rewrites Exodus 21:2–7 to include the release of female Hebrew slaves after six years, which was formerly only possible for males. The second example involves male and female participation in religious feasts. Deuteronomy 16:13–15 appears to rewrite Exodus 23:17 by mentioning women and female slaves, therefore permitting female participation in three important festivals, the Feast of Unleavened Bread, the Feast of Weeks, and the Feast of Booths. Perhaps the most obvious move toward greater egalitarianism is that Deuteronomy 14–15, unlike the Priestly text of Numbers 18, sees tithes and the offering of firstborn animals as something to be enjoyed by all Israelites rather than items that go exclusively to priests and Levites.

Blessings and curses: Deuteronomy 27–8

This section contains a list of blessings for Israel's performance of her covenantal duties and curses for her failure to live out her commitments. As noted in the discussion of contemporary controversies, many believe that the larger structure of Deuteronomy follows a general pattern of ancient Near Eastern treaties between a ruling emperor and smaller territories ruled by a king or a prince. These treaties contained lists of blessings for adherence to the terms of the treaty and curses for failure to do so. In the ancient Near East various divine forces were understood to undergird the social order and were invoked in solemn oaths in much the same way that legal courts in the United States ask those who testify to swear that they will tell the whole truth – 'so help you God' – or when various officials are sworn into office by asking them to recite an oath with their hand on the Bible.

Renewing the covenant: Deuteronomy 29–31

Chapter 29 contains a formal ratification of the covenantal agreement, the terms of which are laid out in the preceding chapters of Deuteronomy. Deuteronomy 30 mirrors aspects of Deuteronomy 4 in that both texts explicitly acknowledge Israel's coming exile and assure the people that if they repent and return to God he will again restore them to the land of Israel. One of the most interesting features of these texts is that they conceive of the covenant as eternally renewable rather than as a contract that once violated is void.

Deuteronomy 31 narrates Moses turning over his position as leader to Joshua, thus making a clear connection to the six historical books that follow the Torah, which record events from Joshua's conquest of the land all the way through the destruction of Jerusalem and the Babylonian exile. It also includes rules for periodic public recitals of the covenantal agreement found in Deuteronomy. Interestingly enough, the Jewish annual reading of the Torah leaves the congregation in the same place as the Israelites in Deuteronomy – standing on the doorstep of the Promised Land, hoping that as they enter into a renewed relationship to God they can this time be obedient to God and receive all the blessings God has intended for them. The Torah, the most sacred scriptural document in Judaism, a document that contains an immense sweep of history, is oriented toward the future.

Moses' last words: Deuteronomy 32–4

Deuteronomy 32 and 33 contain two poems. The first, sometimes called the 'Song of Moses', is a long poem cast as a future prophecy, which includes a recital in broad terms of the history of God's relationship with Israel. The second poetic composition contains Moses' blessing of the various Israelite tribes and is somewhat parallel to Jacob's poem of blessing found in Genesis 49. Deuteronomy 34 begins with the famous scene invoked by Martin Luther King Jr's 'I've been to the mountain top' speech in which Moses is permitted to see but not to enter the Holy Land. It goes on to describe Moses' death and burial and includes a brief statement about Moses' unique qualities as a prophet of the highest order. This statement marks out the revelation of the Torah as unsurpassable, a belief that stands at the very heart of Judaism.

The theme of oneness in Deuteronomy

A recurring theme within the book of Deuteronomy is that of oneness. We have already discussed the *Shema*, the central teaching of Deuteronomy that YHWH, Israel's God, is one, and we noted its importance within Jewish life and prayer as well as the fact that it was not infrequently on the lips of Jews who were martyred. However, there is more to the theme of oneness in Deuteronomy than is communicated in this single passage. Yes, God is one, God is unique, but oneness in Deuteronomy may be seen in at least three other important ways.

The first theme of oneness relates to Israel. According to Deuteronomy 7:6, this people is like no other on the face of the earth in that Israel is chosen by God to be God's treasured possession. The theme of election, the idea that God chose Israel, is developed in Deuteronomy in important ways through its novel and regular use of the Hebrew word *bachar*, meaning 'he chose'. Deuteronomy is careful to specify, however, that Israel's status is *not* due to an inherent moral quality Israel possesses but rather rests purely upon God's love for the Patriarchs and their descendants through Jacob, that is, the people of Israel.

There is also the theme of oneness with regard to the land that Israel will possess; it is considered to be an abundantly good land, a unique land, *the* land that has been promised to Israel as an eternal possession. As a subset of this specific theme, Deuteronomy also places great emphasis on the one 'place the LORD your God shall choose', a place designated in the land in which God will 'put his name' and Israel will worship. It seems clear that this refers to the Jerusalem temple, but the authors exclude the exact location possibly in order to guard against obvious anachronism or perhaps to ease tensions between the rival territories of Judah and Israel over which city, Jerusalem or Samaria, was the specified place.

Finally, there is also a strong sense in Deuteronomy that the teachings given by Moses, this Torah itself, constitute a unique law code that, when enacted, will provide for a good and abundant life, perhaps even leading other nations to recognize the power of Israel's God as suggested in Deuteronomy 4:5–8. It is implied that there are no teachings or law code like it. It is truly the one Torah and when followed, the people will live and worship in the one true way.

The result is remarkable: One God, One People, One Land, One Place, One Torah, One Way. This overarching sense of oneness is attested to on every page of Deuteronomy. This multifaceted theme established in Deuteronomy comes to animate the rest of the Bible.

Examples of Jewish use of Deuteronomy

As noted above, perhaps the most significant Jewish use of Deuteronomy surrounds the *Shema* and the extensive attention paid to issues of loyalty to God and the possible temptations toward idolatry. Of course, there are also a host of laws found in Deuteronomy that have influenced the shape of Jewish societies over thousands of years. A particular legal trend found in Deuteronomy that is worthy of comment is the tendency to give a rationale for quite a number of commandments, and often a rationale that one might call broadly humanistic. Such explanations of the commandments can be found in earlier Israelite legislation such as in Exodus 20:12, where honoring one's parents is linked to the statement that one should do so 'so that your days may be long in the land that the Lord your God is giving you' (found here in Deuteronomy 5:16). But one finds a growing list of commandments similarly grounded in Deuteronomy. These include the following laws: the prohibition on eating animal blood in 12:25; the call to set up a just system of courts in 16:20; a limited kingship in 17:20; and honesty in business dealings in 25:13–16. The drive to seek out explanations for the *mitzvot*, the commandments, plays an important part in post-biblical Jewish thinking, perhaps most obviously evident in the Jewish medieval philosophical quest to explain Jewish belief and practice in rational terms.

Another important aspect of the later Jewish use of Deuteronomy is the way in which the Jewish tradition resolves apparent contradictions in the biblical legislation. While scholars think Deuteronomy contains laws that conflict with other legislation in the Torah, the Jewish tradition has found ways to ease these apparent tensions and to read all of the laws as flowing from a single divine source. Take for example the famous legal midrash which attempts to explain the apparent tension between the Sabbath law's rationale in Exodus 20 and Deuteronomy 5. Exodus 20 speaks of remembering the Sabbath because God rested on the seventh day after creating the world, while Deuteronomy 5 speaks of observing the Sabbath and links this to Israel's Egyptian bondage and the Exodus experience.

The ancient Rabbis, on the basis of a very creative type of biblical interpretation, imagine that God actually spoke to the Israelites at Mount Sinai in a stereophonic fashion; that is, both forms of the law were spoken at the same time. The subtle differences in the language between the Sabbath command in Exodus and Deuteronomy are thereby acknowledged, and given equal authority. In fact, the Rabbis use this principle to derive a custom about how one should both *remember* the Sabbath by beginning it early and one should extend the Sabbath later into the evening of Saturday night by *observing* it after it has officially ended. Thus they assume that God slightly varied the language of this commandment to teach the Jewish community the full meaning of keeping the Sabbath.

HEBREW MATTERS: 'INCISE THEM INTO YOUR CHILDREN'

In the English of Deuteronomy 6:7 one often finds translations such as 'Recite them to your children'. The New Jewish Publication Society translation attempts to capture a bit of the Hebrew flavor with 'Impress them upon your children'. However, the Hebrew verb *shinantam* used here is quite rare and could also be translated as 'incise them [the words that God is commanding Israel] into your children'. The noun for the word 'tooth' in Hebrew is derived from this same verbal root, and a tooth is an object with sharpened edges. Thus the verb seems to carry more force than simply reciting. It implies a type of deep imprinting and to accomplish this one must 'talk about them when you are at home and when you are away, when you lie down and when you rise. Bind them as a sign on your hand, fix them as an emblem on your forehead, and write them on the doorposts of your house and on your gates' (Deuteronomy 6:7–9). As noted earlier, a number of Jewish rituals are derived from this passage, including: the regular recital of the *Shema*, wearing *tefillin*, and the mounting of a *mezuzah* on doorposts (see figures 4

> ### HEBREW MATTERS: 'INCISE THEM INTO YOUR CHILDREN' (cont.)
>
> and 11). One can glimpse the genius of the authors of the Torah who realized that physical reminders are a highly effective way to pass the Torah on to future generations.

Examples of Christian use of Deuteronomy

In addition to Jesus' affirmation that the *Shema* is the most important commandment, Christian use of Deuteronomy may be seen in two important, albeit subtle, ways. The first is found in the idea of community, or chosen people. The full-blown idea of God choosing Israel as found in Deuteronomy is assumed by the authors of the New Testament, yet, according to Paul in Romans 9–11, Gentiles who are 'in Christ' are grafted into Israel through a mysterious process. The promises made to Israel cannot be broken ('they are irrevocable' according to Paul), but the definition of Israel – those who descend from Abraham – is expanded to allow non-Israelites to join this people; these non-Israelites too share in Israel's election in some way. Entrance into this people entails responsibility to God, each other, and the world. The early Church, in practicing this way of life, came to be known as those who lived according to 'the way' (Greek *he hodos*, used in the book of Acts regularly). This communal way of life, in which property is equitably shared (to benefit those in need) and strict moral standards are upheld, resembles much of the teachings so central to Deuteronomy.

Along these lines, a second Christian use of Deuteronomy is related to the orphan and widow. One might argue that Jesus' care for the widow, stranger, poor, and outcast stems from a proper understanding of the Torah as stipulated in Deuteronomy. In caring for those on the margins of society, Jesus signaled a time and place he called the 'Kingdom of God' (or 'Kingdom of Heaven'). It could be argued that Deuteronomy holds a similar vision in that a place is to be formed (the Promised Land) in which the people of Israel thrive, wherein there is no hunger or want, and where God is with his people. One could say that the New Testament's vision of a Kingdom of God owes much to the Torah's – especially Deuteronomy's – vision of how Israel is to live under God and with each other. Here one should recognize the strong resemblance of this vision to the one presented in Leviticus. Thus, even while these two books sometimes differ on specifics, they both strive to create a community that lives in accord with God's will and both books affirm that doing so allows God to dwell in the midst of his chosen people.

Conclusion

Deuteronomy ends the Torah, but it is really also a book of beginnings. We noted above the debate about whether Deuteronomy should belong to the Torah or to the Deuteronomistic History, and in some ways this points to the fact that the authors of Deuteronomy, and those who shaped the rest of the Hebrew Bible, were skillful in their work. They wove together a collection of writings that became closely linked and cannot be separated. Deuteronomy stands together with the rest of the Bible in important ways.

Deuteronomy ends by reporting Moses' death and by highlighting the uniqueness of his life, a model life from a Jewish perspective. In fact, at major life events Jews commonly say to the person celebrating 'may you live to be 120' recognizing that Moses' lifespan and the life he lived are the ideal. And of course Moses had a profound influence on Jesus and on the subsequent shape of Christianity. Whether Moses actually wrote Deuteronomy is something few scholars today would argue, yet it seems apparent that in some way his fingerprints, whether direct or indirect, have been left on this book. His life and teachings will continue to influence the lives of religious practitioners for ages to come and are likely to have an ongoing impact upon wider Western society.

Concluding reflections

It may be helpful to take a moment to reflect on the ongoing significance of the Torah for Jews, Christians, and other Westerners. We hope the reader has come to appreciate that *how* we approach this literature often affects what we get out of it. The questions we ask and the perspectives we take in reading it may contribute more than we think to the outcome of our interpretations. Although we have covered both secular and religious approaches to the Torah, our decision to discuss religious approaches first, and to include materials about Jewish and Christian uses of the Torah throughout this book, signals our conviction that the Torah is not simply another piece of literature but rather is fundamentally a religious text. Its teachings on life, death, sin, holiness, forgiveness, charity, and love of God deeply affect how Jews and Christians live. Clearly, the Torah's stories, laws, and prayers have had a tremendous influence on each faith community and each tradition's self-understanding.

All evidence suggests that the Torah will remain central for Jews and Judaism into the foreseeable future. Even in synagogues that reject many of the traditional interpretations of various biblical laws and customs, one finds congregants engaging the weekly Torah portion week after week. Liturgically, historically, and culturally Jews are bonded together in their connection to this powerful set of stories and laws and to the Deity that for mysterious reasons chose the Jewish people as the vehicle to bring these books to the world.

While we have noted that there are trends among some Christians that suggest a fading interest in the Torah, we would be remiss if we did not point out that this is far from the whole picture. In the wake of the Holocaust, many Christian denominations have reassessed their relationship to Judaism. In doing so, they often have sought out points of connection – such as the Torah's stories, laws, and common ancestors – with Jews. Further, there are signs that Christian academic interest in the Torah is on the rise, especially regarding how these books contribute to canonical readings of Christian scripture. As we noted regularly throughout this book, many passages in the New Testament build upon the content and theology of the Torah. In fact, the New Testament cannot be understood apart from it.

Of course, a secular person, or persons of other religions, might ask, what does any of this have to do with me? Here we would suggest that there are both historic and contemporary reasons why anyone should be interested in delving more deeply into these books. Historically, they have had immense influence on the socio-political development of the Western world. These influences can be seen in numerous small ways, such as the fact that in many places debtors who declare bankruptcy have their credit restored after seven years (which is drawn from Deuteronomy 15), or that witnesses in court are often asked to swear on a Bible that their testimony is true, an act premised upon the belief that one would be hesitant to break two of the Ten Commandments (taking God's name in vain and bearing false witness). They can also be seen in more fundamental ways, such as in the ideas undergirding the American Declaration of Independence, or in the contemporary drive to establish a set of universal human rights – both of which build upon the insight of Genesis 1 that all humans, male and female, are created in God's image and thus imbued with an inalienable dignity. In fact, what could be fairly called the most radical social change in the United States in the twentieth century, the civil rights struggle, employed texts and metaphors drawn from the Torah, more specifically in this case from the book of Exodus, in highly effective ways. And current debates in the West such as those surrounding abortion, assisted suicide, and gay rights revolve not a little over questions of how to understand and interpret various passages found in the Torah.

All of this is to say nothing of the vast trove of Western art and literature, much of which grew out of reflection upon central biblical texts, many of these located in the Torah. Since cultures continue to add new layers upon older ones, and inevitably draw upon older ideas in ever new ways, the enduring significance of the Torah seems assured. But if the Torah's ideas are to be engaged intelligently, it is essential that all types of Western readers be familiar with its content and the various ways, both for good and for ill, it has been interpreted over thousands of years. With this in mind we hope this modest Beginner's Guide will have provided an entry point for engaging the Torah more deeply.

Glossary

Aggadah Part of Jewish Oral Law. Rabbinic teachings of a narrative type as recorded in the Midrash and Talmud.

Ashkenazim, Ashkenazic Jews who descend from Jewish communities spread throughout Northern Europe. The other (major) group of Jews is Sephardic (see entry below).

Canon A word meaning 'rule' or 'measuring stick'. In biblical studies refers to a set collection of authoritative writings used by a religious group (a collection which may vary from group to group).

Catechism Common in Christianity, catechism usually contains summaries of religious teachings, often in a question-and-answer format, to instruct new and young members in the faith.

Chumash The traditional Jewish designation for the Torah in printed form. Derived from the Hebrew word for five.

Church Fathers Early teachers and bishops of the Christian Church who wrote on matters of doctrine, theology, and biblical interpretation.

Covenant A binding agreement between two (not necessarily equal) parties. In the Bible, covenants are often between God and his people, though these can be made between two people or groups, or between God and all humankind.

Covenant Code This refers to Exodus 21–3, which many scholars believe may be the oldest law code in the Torah.

D The letter used by biblical scholars to signify the source that produced Deuteronomy, dated to the seventh century BCE according to the Documentary Hypothesis. Scholars now speak of this as a 'school', or movement, and believe elements of the D school also edited the six historical books following

Deuteronomy (which many now call the Deuteronomistic History).

Day of Atonement (or Yom Kippur) The most holy day of the year in Judaism, on which Jews partake in daylong fasting and prayer for forgiveness.

Dead Sea Scrolls Biblical, para-biblical, and sectarian texts dating between 200 BCE and 70 CE found in an area near the Dead Sea in Israel (called Qumran) in 1947. This collection contains the oldest manuscripts we currently have of texts from the Hebrew Bible.

Deuteronomistic History See 'D' above.

Documentary Hypothesis A theory about the authorship of the Torah, which ascribes its origins to four main sources (J, E, D, and P). Usually associated with the nineteenth-century German biblical scholar Julius Wellhausen.

E The letter used by biblical scholars to signify the Elohistic source of the Pentateuch, due to this source's tendency to use *Elohim* to refer to God. Often associated with the Northern kingdom of Israel. Originally dated in the 700s BCE according to the Documentary Hypothesis.

Elohim A generic Hebrew word meaning God (or gods) in the Hebrew Bible.

Epistle, epistles A Greek word meaning 'letter'. In Christianity, refers to the letters of the New Testament, whether of Paul, Peter, John, and so on.

Eucharist In Christianity a communal meal of bread and wine, signifying Jesus' broken body and shed blood. Also called the Lord's Supper, Holy Communion, or the Blessed Sacrament.

Exile The period in which Israel and Judah lived outside their homelands due to forced military migration. Israel's exile began in 722 BCE (due to the conquest of its capital, Samaria, by Assyria) and Judah's began in 587 BCE (due to the conquest of its capital, Jerusalem, by Babylon). Biblical scholars typically use 'the exile' to refer to the exile of

Judah to Babylon. Judah's exile lasted until the Edict of Cyrus (538 BCE), which permitted Jews to repopulate their homeland.

Gentile, Gentiles Term used (mainly in Judaism and early Christianity) to designate a non-Jew. 'Gentiles' is simply the Latin word for 'nations', but in biblical studies it refers to non-Jewish nations.

Gospel, gospels A word simply meaning 'good news'. In the singular, used in Christianity to refer to the story of Jesus and salvation through him. In the plural, the term usually refers to the first four books of the New Testament, which tell the story of Jesus (Matthew, Mark, Luke, and John).

Haggadah, Passover Haggadah The religious manual used by Jews in their celebration of Passover.

Halakhah The vast body of Jewish religious law found in the Torah, the Talmud, and other later Jewish texts and commentaries built on biblical and rabbinic precedents.

Hebrew Bible A scholarly designation for the Tanakh, or what Christians call the Old Testament.

Holiness Code This refers to Leviticus 17–26, a block of material that emphasizes both ethics and ritual as a means to holiness.

Israelite, Israeli *Israelite* refers to a member of Israel in *antiquity*. An *Israeli* is a citizen of the *modern* state of Israel.

J The letter used by biblical scholars to signify the YHWHistic source of the Pentateuch, the only source to use the divine name YHWH in Genesis. This Southern (or Judean) source was believed to be the earliest source of the Torah according to the Documentary Hypothesis, originally dated to around 850 BCE.

Jewish Scriptures A designation for the Hebrew Bible or Tanakh, which includes the same books found in the (Christian) Old Testament but in a different order.

Jubilee, Jubilee Year The year in which all lands were to be returned to their original owners, debts were canceled, and all Israelite slaves were freed. Takes place at the end of seven cycles of Sabbatical years, every 49 (or possibly 50) years.

Kosher, kashrut Food determined to be fit for consumption in Judaism, based on Jewish law.

Lection, lectionary A lection is an excerpt of scripture read in a religious context. A lectionary refers to an annual or multiple-year cycle of scriptural readings.

Liturgy, liturgical Related to religious worship or the texts used within worship settings.

Masoretes, Masoretic tradition, Masoretic Text The Masoretes were sixth- to tenth-century CE Jewish scribes who helped stabilize the biblical text. They created a system of vowel and chant markings (called the Masorah) based on the traditions they had inherited concerning how the Torah was to be read and chanted. Their text of the Hebrew Bible, with its markings, is called the Masoretic Text.

Midrash A verse by verse commentary on portions of Jewish scripture. There are two major genres of midrash: midrash halakhah, which comments on legal portions of the Torah (parts of Exodus and most of Leviticus, Numbers, Deuteronomy), and midrash aggadah, which comments on narrative parts of the Tanakh, such as Genesis and the first half of Exodus.

Mishnah A rabbinic legal compilation from around 200 CE. Often scholars speak of it as the first attempt to write down the Oral Torah for fear it would be lost in the wake of the dispersion of the Jews that occurred after the Roman destruction of the second temple in 70 CE.

Mitzvot A Hebrew term for 'commandments'; in the singular, Mitzvah. (Readers may be familiar with the term 'bar/bat Mitzvah', which means 'son/daughter of the commandment'.)

Monolatry The worship of one God while acknowledging that other gods may exist.

Monotheism The belief that only one God exists.

New Testament The second section of the Christian Bible, containing the story of Jesus and other Christian teachings. Generally dated to between 50 CE and 110 CE.

Noahide laws In Judaism, a short list of basic commandments (such as not murdering, not stealing, and not committing adultery) that apply to all humans, that is, those considered to be the 'descendants of Noah'.

Old Testament The Christian designation for the Hebrew Bible. The Old Testament and the Jewish Tanakh contain exactly the same books but in differing order.

Oral Law, Oral Torah In Judaism, those teachings traditionally believed to be handed down orally from Moses at Mount Sinai, which more fully explicate the laws and lore recorded in the Pentateuch.

P The letter used by biblical scholars to signify the Priestly source of the Pentateuch. According to the Documentary Hypothesis, the last piece to be added to the Torah dating from around 450 BCE.

Passover A feast commemorating Israel's Exodus from Egypt, in which God 'passed over' the homes of the Israelites sparing their first-born sons, unlike those of the Egyptians who were killed.

Pentateuch Another name for the Torah or the Five Books of Moses. Comes from Greek words meaning 'five scrolls' or 'five vessels'.

Promised Land The land promised to Abraham by God in the book of Genesis, initially identified as Canaan, later called Israel.

Qur'an The sacred scripture of Islam.

Rabbi Hebrew term for 'teacher'. In this book 'Rabbis' most often refers to ancient teachers of the law in Judaism, Jewish sages who produced the Mishnah, Talmud, and the oldest collections of midrash.

Rule of Faith A core set of Christian teachings that guide the Church's interpretation of scripture.

Scripture A word simply meaning 'writing', often used in antiquity to signify (in its plural form, 'the scriptures') the sacred or authoritative literature of Judaism and Christianity.

Sabbath, Shabbat (sometimes Shabbos) A day of rest taken by religious Jews on Saturday. In Christian contexts, can refer to their weekly day of worship, Sunday.

Sabbath Year The seventh year in which land is to be left fallow, according to Leviticus 25.

Sephardim, Sephardic Jews whose ancestors resided in Spain, Portugal, and the southernmost part of France. The other (major) group of Jews is Ashkenazic (see above).

Sepher The Hebrew word for scroll, often translated as 'book'.

Septuagint A third- to first-century BCE Jewish translation of the Hebrew Bible into Greek. The Septuagint was also the Bible of many early Jesus-followers, including Paul and the churches to whom he wrote letters.

Shema A Hebrew word meaning 'hear' or 'listen'. *Shema* is the first word of Deuteronomy 6:4, which contains an important affirmation of Israel's understanding of God's oneness. This central Jewish prayer is referred to as 'the *Shema*' in Judaism and is the most important commandment in Christianity, according to Jesus.

Shofar Hebrew word for ram's horn, traditionally blown on Rosh Hashanah (Jewish New Year).

Simchat Torah An annual Jewish festival in which each congregation engages in extended dancing with the community's Torah scrolls in celebration of completing the reading of the Torah.

Talmud A wide-ranging rabbinic legal text that was produced between 200 and 700 CE, built around the Mishnah. Thus each Talmudic discussion starts with a section of the Mishnah.

Tanakh An acronym for the Jewish Bible consisting of T for Torah (the Pentateuch), N for Neviim (the Prophets, consisting of six historical books and fifteen books containing prophetic material), and K for Ketuvim (the Writings, or everything else in the Jewish Bible).

Vulgate A Latin translation of the Christian Bible, completed by St Jerome in the early fifth century CE.

Written Law, Written Torah A Jewish designation for the Torah in written form (as opposed to 'Oral Law'; see above).

YHWH The personal, covenantal name of Israel's God. The exact vowels, and thus pronunciation, are unknown (see pp. 44–45 above).

Yom Kippur See 'Day of Atonement'.

Timeline (all dates are approximate)

1800 BCE = Abraham.

1280 BCE = The Exodus from Egypt.

1240 BCE = The Conquest of Canaan.

1020 BCE = King Saul, Israel's first monarch.

1000 BCE = King David.

960 BCE = King Solomon, who built the Jerusalem temple.

922 BCE = The once United Kingdom splits into two: the North (Israel, or Ephraim) and the South (Judah).

722 BCE = The Northern Kingdom (Israel) falls when it is conquered by Assyria (Israel goes into exile).

587 BCE = The Southern Kingdom (Judah) falls when it is conquered by Babylonia (Judah is exiled).

538 BCE = The Edict of Cyrus (the Persian Emperor) allows the Judean exiles to return and rebuild the temple. This begins the Second Temple Period.

400 BCE = The Torah is compiled into its final form.

333 BCE = Alexander the Great conquers the Persian empire and takes all its holdings, including what was once the territory of biblical Israel.

250 BCE = The Tanakh is translated into Greek, resulting in the Septuagint.

160 BCE = The Maccabees achieve semi-autonomous status for the territory of Judah.

63 BCE = Pompey, a Roman general, takes Jerusalem.

5 BCE = Jesus is born (the exact date is debated).

(continued overleaf)

70 CE = The second temple and Jerusalem are destroyed by the Romans.

110 CE = The final books of the New Testament are completed.

200 CE = The Mishnah is compiled.

Sources and further reading

As noted in our introductory comments, this book is intended to draw the reader into the text of the Torah, and the vast array of interpretations to which it has given birth over thousands of years. With this in mind, we hope the reader will pursue further study of the Torah. To facilitate this process we have included suggestions for further reading on each chapter of our book. We also strongly recommend that those who have the time and inclination consider taking a college level or adult education course offered by a university, a church, or a synagogue. One of the best ways to learn more about the Torah is to do so in a larger group with a knowledgeable teacher.

Readers may also be interested to know that many Bibles today include essays and other helpful tools such as maps and charts to help the lay reader gain a deeper knowledge of the Torah. For example, the *New Oxford Annotated Bible* has a College Edition Study Bible with much helpful material. The *New Interpreter's Study Bible* is full of theologically engaging notes and essays, from a Christian perspective. The *Etz Hayim* and *Jewish Study Bible* are also excellent resources. There are also major reference works on all things biblical such as the *Anchor Bible Dictionary*, *The Dictionary of the Old Testament: Pentateuch*, and the *New Interpreter's Dictionary of the Bible*. We list these and others below (see especially the resources under chapter 1 as well as 'Concluding reflections'). Note that many of these dictionaries contain short articles on topics of interest and will point you to yet further readings.

Note: In places below we provide more than one heading per chapter, in order to organize things more effectively, particularly where more than one topic or divergent topics are discussed within any one chapter.

Chapter 1: A few basics

Study Bibles and translations of the Torah

The Jewish Study Bible: JPS Tanakh Translation. Edited by Adele Berlin et al. New York: Oxford University Press, 2004.

Etz Hayim: Torah and Commentary. Edited by David L. Lieber and Jules Harlow. Philadelphia: Jewish Publication Society, 2001.

The New Interpreter's Study Bible. Edited by Walter J. Harrelson. Nashville: Abingdon, 2003.

The HarperCollins Study Bible. Revised edition. Edited by Harold W. Attridge et al. New York: HarperCollins, 2006.

The New Oxford Annotated Bible. Fourth edition. Edited by Michael D. Coogan et al. London: Oxford University Press, 2010.

The Catholic Study Bible. Second edition. Edited by Donald Senior and John J. Collins. New York: Oxford University Press, 2006.

Alter, Robert. *The Five Books of Moses: A Translation and Commentary*. New York: Norton & Co., 2004.

Fox, Everett. *The Five Books of Moses: A New Translation with Introductions, Commentary, and Notes*. New York: Schocken Books, 1995.

Scrolls, language, and versions

Danker, Frederick W. *Multipurpose Tools for Bible Study*. Second edition. Minneapolis: Fortress Press, 2003.

Toorn, Karel van der. *Scribal Culture and the Making of the Hebrew Bible*. Cambridge: Harvard University Press, 2007.

Tov, Emanuel. *Textual Criticism of the Hebrew Bible*. Second revised edition. Minneapolis: Fortress, 2001.

Chapter 2: The Torah as a religious book

Traditional Jewish interpretation of the Torah

Brettler, Marc Z. *How to Read the Bible*. Philadelphia: Jewish Publication Society, 2005.

Kugel, James L. *The Bible As It Was*. Cambridge, MA: Belknap Press of Harvard University Press, 1997.

Traditional Christian interpretation of the Torah

Grant, Robert M. with David Tracy. *A Short History of the Interpretation of the Bible*. Revised edition. Minneapolis: Fortress Press, 2005.

Hall, Christopher A. *Reading Scripture with the Church Fathers*. Downers Grove, IL: InterVarsity Press, 1998.

Kannengiesser, Charles. *Handbook of Patristic Exegesis: The Bible in Ancient Christianity* (volume 1). Leiden: Brill, 2004.

Kugel, James L. and Rowan A. Greer. *Early Biblical Interpretation*. Philadelphia: Westminster Press, 1986.

O'Keefe, John J. and R. R. Reno. *Sanctified Vision: An Introduction to Early Christian Interpretation of the Bible*. Baltimore: John Hopkins University Press, 2005.

The Torah and Islam

Abdel Haleem, M. A. S. *The Qur'an*. Oxford: Oxford University Press, 2004.

Solomon, N., Richard Harries, and Tim Winter (eds). *Abraham's Children: Jews, Christians, and Muslims in Conversation*. London: T&T Clark, 2006.

Chapter 3: Modern approaches to the Torah

Overviews of approaches

Barton, John (ed). *The Cambridge Companion to Biblical Interpretation*. Cambridge: Cambridge University Press, 1998.

Rogerson, John W. and Judith M. Lieu (eds). *The Oxford Handbook of Biblical Studies*. Oxford: Oxford University Press, 2008.

Soulen, Richard N. and R. Kendall Soulen. *Handbook of Biblical Criticism*. Third edition. Louisville: Westminster John Knox Press 2001.

Historical criticism

Collins, John J. *The Bible after Babel: Historical Criticism in a Postmodern Age*. Grand Rapids: Eerdmans, 2005.

Krentz, Edgar. *The Historical-Critical Method*. Philadelphia: Fortress Press, 1975. Reprinted by Wipf & Stock Publishers, 2002.

Levenson, Jon D. *The Hebrew Bible, the Old Testament, and Historical Criticism: Jews and Christians in Biblical Studies*. Louisville: Westminster John Knox, 1993.

On authorship and Pentateuchal sources

Blenkinsopp, Joseph. *The Pentateuch: An Introduction to the First Five Books of the Bible*. New York: Doubleday, 1992.

Friedman, Richard Elliot. *Who Wrote the Bible?* New York: Harper-Collins, 1997.

Wenham, Gordon J. *Exploring the Old Testament: A Guide to the Pentateuch*. Downers Grove, IL: InterVarsity Press, 2003.

Text box: The names of God

Seitz, Christopher R. *Word without End: The Old Testament as Abiding Theological Witness*. Louisville: Westminster John Knox, 2001. (See pp. 131–44.)

Van Wijk-Bos, Johanna W. H. 'Writing on the water: the ineffable name of God', in Alice Ogden Bellis and Joel S. Kaminsky (eds). *Jews, Christians, and the Theology of the Hebrew Scriptures*, pp. 45–59. Atlanta: Society of Biblical Literature, 2000.

On history, archeology, and the Torah ('minimalist')

Davies, Philip R. *In Search Of 'Ancient Israel'*. Second edition. Sheffield: Sheffield Academic, 1995.

Thompson, Thomas L. *The Historicity of the Patriarchal Narratives: The Quest for the Historical Abraham*. Harrisburg, PA: Trinity Press International, 2002.

On history, archeology, and the Torah ('moderate')

Day, John (ed). *In Search of Pre-exilic Israel: Proceedings of the Oxford Old Testament Seminar*. London: T&T Clark, 2004.

Dever, William G. *What Did the Biblical Writers Know and When Did they Know It? What Archaeology Can Tell Us About the Reality of Ancient Israel*. Grand Rapids: Eerdmans, 2002.

Miller, J. Maxwell and John H. Hayes. *A History of Ancient Israel and Judah*. Second edition. Louisville: Westminster John Knox, 2006.

On history, archeology, and the Torah ('maximalist')

Bright, John. *A History of Israel: With an Introduction and Appendix by William P. Brown*. Fourth edition. Louisville: Westminster John Knox Press, 2000.

Provan, Iain, V. Philips Long and Tremper Longman. *A Biblical History of Israel*. Louisville: Westminster John Knox, 2003.

Feminist approaches

Brenner, Athalya (ed). *Exodus to Deuteronomy: A Feminist Companion to the Bible* (second series). Sheffield: Sheffield Academic Press, 2000.

Brenner, Athalya (ed). *Genesis: A Feminist Companion the Bible* (second series). Sheffield: Sheffield Academic Press, 1998.

Eskenazi, Tamara Cohn and Andrea L. Weiss (eds). *The Torah: A Women's Commentary*. New York: URJ Press, 2008.

Frymer-Kensky, Tikva. *Reading the Women of the Bible: A New Interpretation of Their Stories*. New York: Shocken Books. 2002.

Loades, Ann. 'Feminist interpretation', in John Barton (ed) *The Cambridge Companion to Biblical Interpretation*, pp. 81–94. Cambridge: Cambridge University Press, 1998.

Myers, Carol. *Discovering Eve: Ancient Israelite Women in Context*. Oxford: Oxford University Press, 1988.

Taylor, Marion Ann and Heather E. Weir. *Let Her Speak for Herself: Nineteenth-Century Women Writing on Women in Genesis*. Waco: Baylor University Press, 2006.

Trible, Phyllis. *God and the Rhetoric of Sexuality*. Philadelphia: Augsburg Fortress, 1978.

Socio-political and ideological

Brett, Mark G. *Genesis: Procreation and the Politics of Identity*. London/New York: Routledge, 2000.

Carter, Charles E. and Carol L. Meyers (eds). *Community, Identity, and Ideology: Social Science Approaches to the Hebrew Bible*. Winona Lake, IN: Eisenbrauns, 1996.

Clines, David J. A. *Interested Parties: The Ideology of Writers and Readers of the Hebrew Bible*. Sheffield: Sheffield Academic Press, 1995.

Gottwald, Norman K. *The Tribes of YHWH: A Sociology of the Religion of Liberated Israel, 1250–1030 BCE*. London: SCM Press, 1980.

Heard, R. Christopher. *Dynamics of Diselection: Ambiguity in Genesis 12–36 and Ethnic Boundaries in Post-Exilic Judah*. Atlanta: SBL, 2001.

Levenson, Jon D. *The Death and Resurrection of the Beloved Son: The Transformation of Child Sacrifice in Judaism and Christianity*. New Haven: Yale University Press, 1993.

Pleins, David J. *The Social Visions of the Hebrew Bible: A Theological Introduction*. Louisville: Westminster John Knox, 2001.

Sperling, S. David. *The Original Torah: The Political Intent of the Bible's Writers*. New York: New York University Press, 1998.

Literary criticism

Alter, Robert. *The Art of Biblical Narrative*. New York: Basic Books, 1981.

Alter, Robert and Frank Kermode (eds). *The Literary Guide to the Bible*. Cambridge: Belknap Press of Harvard University Press, 1987.

Bar-Efrat, Shimon. *Narrative Art in the Bible*. Translated by Dorothea Shefer-Vanson. Second edition. Sheffield: Sheffield Academic Press, 1989.

Berlin, Adele. *Poetics and Biblical Interpretation*. Sheffield: Almond Press, 1983.

Fokkelman, J. P. *Reading Biblical Narrative: An Introductory Guide*. Translated by Ineke Smit. Louisville: Westminster John Knox Press, 1999.

Ryken, Leland and Tremper Longman III (eds). *A Complete Literary Guide to the Bible*. Grand Rapids: Zondervan, 1993.

Canonical and theological

Brett, Mark G. *Biblical Criticism in Crisis? The Impact of the Canonical Approach on Old Testament Studies*. Cambridge: Cambridge University Press, 1991.

Childs, Brevard S. *Introduction to the Old Testament as Scripture*. Philadelphia: Fortress, 1979.

Treier, Daniel. *Introducing Theological Interpretation of Scripture: Recovering a Christian Practice*. Grand Rapids: Baker Academic, 2008.

Chapter 4: Genesis

Brueggemann, Walter. *Genesis*. Atlanta: John Knox, 1982.

Fretheim, Terence. *Abraham: Trials of Family and Faith*. Columbia, SC: University of South Carolina, 2007.

Kaminsky, Joel S. *Yet I Loved Jacob: Reclaiming the Biblical Concept of Election*. Nashville: Abingdon, 2007.

Moberly, R. W. L. *The Theology of the Book of Genesis*. Cambridge: Cambridge University Press, 2009.

Origen, *On First Principles*. Translated by G. W. Butterworth. New York: Harper & Row, 1966.

Sarna, Nahum M. *The JPS Torah Commentary: Genesis*. Philadelphia: Jewish Publication Society, 1989.

Chapter 5: Exodus

Brueggemann, Walter. 'The Book of Exodus', in Leander E. Keck (ed). *New Interpreter's Bible*. Nashville: Abingdon, 1994.

Childs, Brevard S. *The Book of Exodus: A Critical, Theological Commentary*. Louisville: Westminster, 1974.

Fretheim, Terence. *Exodus*. Louisville: John Knox, 1991.

Lierman, John. *The New Testament Moses: Christian Perceptions of Moses and Israel in the Setting of Jewish Religion*. Tubingen: Mohr Siebeck, 2004.

Moberly, R. W. L. *At the Mountain of God: Story and Theology in Exodus 32–34*. Sheffield: JSOT Press, 1983.

Sarna, Nahum M. *The JPS Torah Commentary: Exodus*. Philadelphia: Jewish Publication Society, 1991.

Chapter 6: Leviticus

Douglas, Mary. *Leviticus as Literature*. Oxford: Oxford University Press, 1999.

Douglas, Mary. *Purity and Danger: An Analysis of the Concepts of Pollution and Taboo*. London: Routledge, 1966.

Hendel, Ronald S. 'Table and Altar: The Anthropology of Food in the Priestly Torah', in Robert B. Coote and Norman K. Gottwald (eds). *To Break Every Yoke: Essays in Honor of Marvin L. Chaney*, pp. 131–48. Sheffield: Sheffield Phoenix Press, 2007.

Klawans, Jonathan. *Impurity and Sin in Ancient Judaism*. Oxford: Oxford University Press, 2000.

Levine, Baruch A. *The JPS Torah Commentary: Leviticus*. Philadelphia: Jewish Publication Society, 1989.

Milgrom, Jacob. *Leviticus: A Book of Ritual and Ethics*. Minneapolis: Fortress Press, 2004.

Wenham, Gordon J. *The Book of Leviticus*. Grand Rapids: Eerdmans, 1979.

Chapter 7: Numbers

Levine, Baruch A. *Numbers 1–20: A New Translation with Introduction and Commentary*. New York: Doubleday, 1993.

Levine, Baruch A. *Numbers 21–36: A New Translation with Introduction and Commentary*. New York: Doubleday, 2000.

Milgrom, Jacob. *The JPS Torah Commentary: Numbers*. Philadelphia: Jewish Publication Society, 1990.

Olson, Dennis T. *The Death of the Old and the Birth of the New: The Framework of the Book of Numbers and the Pentateuch*. Chico, CA: Scholars Press, 1985.

Chapter 8: Deuteronomy

Levinson, Bernard M. *Deuteronomy and the Hermeneutics of Legal Innovation*. Oxford: Oxford University Press, 2002.

MacDonald, Nathan. *Deuteronomy and the Meaning of 'Monotheism'*. Tübingen: Mohr Siebeck, 2003.

Miller, Patrick D. *Deuteronomy*. Louisville: John Knox, 1991.

Nicholson, Ernest W. *Deuteronomy and Tradition*. Oxford: Blackwell, 1967.

Olson, Dennis T. *Deuteronomy and the Death of Moses: A Theological Reading*. Minneapolis: Fortress, 1994.

Tigay, Jeffrey H. *The JPS Torah Commentary: Deuteronomy*. Philadelphia: Jewish Publication Society, 1996.

Weinfeld, Moshe. *Deuteronomy 1–11: A New Translation with Introduction and Commentary*. New York: Doubleday, 1991.

Concluding reflections

General reading and more detailed introductions to the Torah

Clines, David J. A. *The Theme of the Pentateuch*. Second edition. Sheffield: Sheffield Academic Press, 1997.

Fretheim, Terence E. *The Pentateuch*. Nashville: Abingdon, 1996.

Ska, Jean Louis. *Introduction to Reading the Pentateuch*. Winona Lake, IN: Eisenbrauns, 2006.

Van Wijk-Bos, Johanna W. H. *Making Wise the Simple: The Torah in Christian Faith and Practice*. Grand Rapids: Eerdmans, 2005.

Wenham, Gordon J. *Exploring the Old Testament: A Guide to the Pentateuch*. Downers Grove, IL: InterVarsity Press, 2003.

Whybray, R. N. *Introduction to the Pentateuch*. Grand Rapids: Eerdmans, 1995.

Dictionaries related to the Torah and its interpretation

The Anchor Bible Dictionary. 6 volumes. Edited by David Noel Freedman. New York: Doubleday, 1992.

Dictionary of Biblical Criticism and Interpretation. Edited by Stanley E. Porter. London: Routledge, 2009.

Dictionary of the Old Testament: Pentateuch. Edited by T. Desmond Alexander and David W. Baker. Downers Grove, IL: Inter-Varsity, 2003.

New Interpreter's Dictionary of the Bible. 5 volumes. Edited by Katharine Doob Sakenfeld. Nashville: Abingdon, 2007.

The SCM Dictionary of Biblical Interpretation. Edited by R. J. Coggins and J. L. Houlden. London: SCM Press, 2003.

Subject Index

Note: Page numbers for illustrations are shown in italics.

References Index

A Beginner's Guide to Christianity

978-1-85168-539-4
£9.99/14.95

Renowned theologian and bestselling author Keith Ward provides an original and authoritative introduction for those seeking a deeper understanding of this complex faith.

"Well ordered and clearly written. Will quickly become a standard textbook." *Theology*

"An articulate presentation of diverse approaches to Christianity's central concerns ... highly recommended." *Library Journal*

KEITH WARD is Professor of Divinity at Gresham College, London and Regius Professor of Divinity Emeritus, at the University of Oxford. A Fellow of the British Academy and an ordained priest in the Church of England, he has authored many books on the topics of Christianity, faith, and science including the best-selling *God: A Guide for the Perplexed* and *The Case for Religion*, both published by Oneworld.

Browse further titles at
www.oneworld-publications.com

A Beginner's Guide to Judaism

Examining the faith as a religion, philosophy, and lifestyle, this authoritative introduction asks what it means to be Jewish today. From the nature of God to worship and everyday life, Dan and Lavinia Cohn-Sherbok address the topics essential to an informed understanding of this highly influential religion.

978-1-85168-748-0
£9.99

"A superb introduction to the central beliefs and cultural expressions of Jews from biblical times to the present day." **Suzannah Heschel** – Eli Black Professor of Jewish Studies, Dartmouth College, USA

"If you are interested in Jewish history but also want to understand the controversies surrounding Jewish life today, then this is where to start." **Marc Ellis** – University Professor of Jewish Studies and Director of the Center for Jewish Studies, Baylor University, USA

DAN COHN-SHERBOK was Professor of Judaism at the University of Wales, and is the author or editor of over 80 books.

LAVINIA COHN-SHERBOK is a writer specialising in Judaism and Jewish issues, a published novelist, and a former headmistress.

Browse further titles at
www.oneworld-publications.com

A Beginner's Guide to The Qur'an

978-1-85168-624-7
£9.99/ $14.95

Drawing on both contemporary and ancient sources, Esack outlines the key themes and explains the historical and cultural context of this unique work whilst examining its content, language, and style, and the variety of approaches used to interpret it.

"Extremely learned yet accessible, with fascinating insights on virtually every page. Especially useful for those new to the study of Islam, or newly interested in their inherited Islam. Its clarity makes it suitable for undergraduates but its sophistication makes it of interest to graduates as well." **Tamara Sonn** – Kenan Professor of Humanities at the College of William and Mary, Virginia

"No one has placed the Noble Qur'an more fully in its historical and contemporary context. Esack's is a user's guide for all users, and it should enjoy a long shelf life as the most accessible, and informative, introduction to God's Word in Arabic." **Bruce Lawrence** – Nancy and Jeffrey Marcus Professor of Religion, Duke University

FARID ESACK has an international reputation as a Muslim scholar, speaker, and human rights activist. He has lectured widely on religion and Islamic Studies and also served as a Commissioner for Gender Equality in Nelson Mandela's government.

A Beginner's Guide to Philosophy of Religion

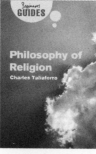

Assuming no prior knowledge of philosophy from the reader, Taliaferro provides a clear exploration of the discipline, introducing a wide range of philosophers and covering the topics of morality and religion, evil, the afterlife, prayer, and miracles.

9781851686506
£9.99/ $14.95

"Brimming with arguments, the material is cutting edge, and the selection of topics is superb."
J.P. Moreland – Professor of Philosophy, St Olaf College, Minnesota

"Covers all the most important issues in a way that is always fair-minded, and manages to be accessible without over-simplifying" **John Cottingham** – President of the British Society for the Philosophy of Religion and Professor Emeritus of Philosophy, Reading University

CHARLES TALIAFERRO is Professor of Philosophy at St. Olaf College, Minnesota, USA. He is the author or editor of numerous books on the philosophy of religion including as co-editor of *The Blackwell Companion to Philosophy of Religion*.

Browse further titles at
www.oneworld-publications.com

A Beginner's Guide to the Baha'i Faith

Moojan Momen
Baha'i Faith

GUIDES

This comprehensive study gives anyone interested in the contemporary religious landscape an authoritative insight into this 150-year old tradition, whose spiritual and social teachings are so much in tune with the concerns of today.

978-1-85168-563-9
£9.99/ $14.95

Who founded the Baha'i Faith?

What do the Baha'i teachings say will bring us happiness and contentment?

What is the Baha'i view on the purpose of life?

How do Baha'i teachings relate to twenty-first century living?

DR MOOJAN MOMEN has lectured at many universities on topics in Middle Eastern studies and religious studies. He is a Fellow of the Royal Asiatic Society and the author of many books on world religions including *Baha'u'llah: A Short Biography*, also published by Oneworld.

Beginners
GUIDES

A Beginner's Guide to The Buddha

978-1-85168-601-8
£9.99/ $14.95

In this authoritative biography, John Strong presents the Buddha's story the way Buddhists have told it – from accounts of his previous lives, and the story of his birth and upbringing, through to his enlightenment, deathbed deeds, and ongoing presence in the relics that he left behind.

"Among the many biographies of the Buddha available to the general reader, John Strong's remains the best. It draws from a vast body of sources with sensitivity and insight to paint a fascinating portrait of a towering figure." **Donald S. Lopez** – Arthur E. Link Distinguished University Professor of Buddhist and Tibetan Studies, University of Michigan

"Strong's book is clearly the best available 'Guide for Beginners'." **Frank Reynolds** – Professor Emeritus of History of Religions and Buddhist Studies, University of Chicago

JOHN S. STRONG is Charles A. Dana Professor of Religious Studies at Bates College in Maine, USA. He is the author of four other books on Buddhism.

Browse further titles at
www.oneworld-publications.com

A Beginner's Guide to Humanism

978-1-85168-589-9
£9.99/ $14.95

Showing how humanists make sense of the world using reason, experience, and sensitivity, Cave emphasizes that we can, and should, flourish without God. Lively, provocative, and refreshingly rant-free, this book is essential reading for all – whether atheist, agnostic, believer, or of no view – who wish better to understand what it means to be human.

"An admirable guide for all those non-religious who may wake up to the fact that they are humanists." **Sir Bernard Crick** – Emeritus Professor of Birkbeck College, University of London, and author of *Democracy: A Very Short Introduction*

"Humanism is loving, sharing and caring and above all an intelligent philosophical way to make the best of our own and our neighbours' lives. I could not commend it more." **Clare Rayner** – Broadcaster, writer and Vice President of the British Humanist Association

Writer and broadcaster Peter Cave teaches philosophy for The Open University and City University London. Author of the bestselling *Can A Robot Be Human?,* he chairs the Humanist Philosophers' Group, frequently contributes to philosophy journals and magazines, and has presented several philosophy programmes for the BBC. He lives in London.

Browse further titles at
www.oneworld-publications.com

A Beginner's Guide to Islamic Philosophy

978-1-85168-625-4
£9.99

Tracing the history of the interactions of philosophy, theology, and mysticism in Islamic culture, Majid Fakhry's comprehensive survey follows the evolution of thought from the introduction of Greek philosophy into the Muslim world in the eighth century right up to the modern era.

"Provides the reader with an excellent, concise overview of Islamic philosophy, theology, and mysticism ... Fakhry has accomplished the task of presenting the central themes and the essence of 1400 years of intellectual tradition in a clear, coherent manner."
Philosophy East and West

MAJID FAKHRY is Emeritus Professor of Philosophy at the American University of Beirut, and formerly Lecturer at SOAS, University of London, Visiting Professor at UCLA, and Associate Professor of Philosophy, Georgetown University. His publications include *A History of Islamic Philosophy* (Columbia University Press), *The Qur'an: A Modern English Version* (Garnet), *Ethical Theories in Islam* (Brill), *Averroes: His Life, Works, and Influence*, and *Al-Farabi, Founder of Islamic Neoplatonism* (both Oneworld).

Browse further titles at
www.oneworld-publications.com

A Beginner's Guide to Hinduism

In his sweeping exploration of the origins, beliefs, scriptures, and modern challenges of Hinduism, Klaus K. Klostermaier captures the diversity at the heart of this complex and esoteric religion.

978-1-85168-538-7
£9.99

"It is immensely readable, works well as an introduction, but will also challenge and intrigue the academic and devotee alike."
World Faiths Encounter

"Easy to read and hard to put down." **Harold Coward** – Professor of History and Founding Director of the Centre for Studies in Religion and Society, University of Victoria

KLAUS K. KLOSTERMAIER, Fellow of the Royal Society of Canada, is University Distinguished Professor Emeritus in the Department of Religious Studies at the University of Manitoba in Canada. He is the author of many books including *A Concise Encyclopedia of Hinduism* and *Buddhism: A Short Introduction* both published by Oneworld.

Browse further titles at
www.oneworld-publications.com